Jacques Arr

ST. MARTIN DE PORRES:

IN THE SERVICE OF COMPASSION

Translated by
George G. Christian, OP

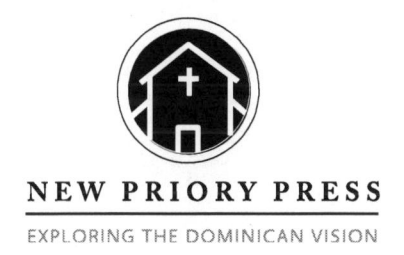

NEW PRIORY PRESS
EXPLORING THE DOMINICAN VISION

New Priory Press acknowledges with gratitude permission for the English edition of *Saint Martin de Porres Au Service de la Compassion* granted by Jacques Ambec, O.P., and the Dominican Province of Toulouse, May 30, 2015.

Copyright © 2015 by the Dominican Province of St. Albert the Great (U.S.A.) All rights reserved. Published by New Priory Press,
1910 South Ashland Avenue, Chicago, IL 60608-2903
NewPrioryPress.com

Table of Contents

Dedication v
Author's Notes vii
Preface ix
Introduction xiii

CHAPTER ONE 1
1. Birth and Childhood of Martin 1
2. The Vocation of Martin: In the Footsteps of St. Dominic .. 7
3. Brother to the Poor: Martin of Charity 12
4. The Extent of Brother Martin's Charity 19
5. The Mortifications of Brother Martin 24
6. The Marvelous Displacements of Martin 29
7. Martin's Other Miracles 35

CHAPTER TWO 43
1. The Holy Death of Brother Martin 43
2. The Canonization of Brother Martin de Porres 53
3. Texts Proposed for the Office of Lessons on 3 November, Feast Day of St. Martin de Porres 61

CHAPTER THREE 65
1. Blessed Simon Ballachi (1250-1319) Soldier, Vegetable Grower, Visionary 65
2. Blessed James of Ulm (1407-1491)- Stained-glass Maker, Mercenary, Fortunate Artist 67
3. St. Juan (John) Macias (1585-1645) - Lay-brother of St. Magdalen Convent in Lima 69
4. The Canonization of John Macias in Rome 92

APPENDICES 99
1. History and Phraseology of the Word: "Lay-brother" to "Cooperator Brother" 99
2. The Cooperator Brother Today 105
3. The Proclamation of the Gospel of Life 113

Table of Prayers

1. God Directs Us 6
2. Vocation 11
3. The mission of love 18
4. Compassion 23
5. Repentance 28
6. The Gifts from God 34
7. The Christian Calling 42
8. At the Hour of Our Death 52
9. The Glory of God 60
10. It Is the Living Man 64
11. Prayer to St. John Macias: Perfect Charity 91
12. For Vocations 105
13. Prayer of Welcome: With a Smile 108
14. Daily Prayer to St. Martin de Porres 109
15. Prayer of Bruno: for Visit to a Sick Person 113
16. Prayer to Mary of Pope John Paul II with AIDS Patients 118

Dedication

To Friar Dominique Frémin in honor of his 80 years. He received me into the Order of Friars Preachers and was the Father Master during the five years of formation to the Dominican religious life, from 1968 to 1974, at the convent of Toulouse.

After the Vatican II Council had given to consecrated religious life its authentic place, especially for religious not ordained, by a return to the sources of their founder so as to give full value to their vocation, Friar Dominique Frémin created the center for the formation of Cooperator Brothers in Toulouse in 1964.

To all the Cooperator Brothers of the Order of Friars Preachers who wish to follow in the footsteps of St. Dominic in the manner of St. Martin de Porres, our model and patron saint.

Author's Notes

In the life of St. Martin de Porres, we find three loves: **Christ Crucified, Our Lady of the Rosary,** and **St. Dominic.** Three passions inflamed his heart and guided his religious life: **compassion**, especially for the sick, the poor, those in need; most rigorous **mortification**, which he considered "the price of love"; and, giving inspiration to the virtues, **humility**, which animated his entire religious life in the service of his brothers and of his neighbor.

Friar Dominique Frémin was Father Master of Novices and charged with the formation of Cooperator Brothers at the convent of Toulouse, from 1962 to 1974. He wrote an article, at the request of Father Baron, Director of the *Revue du Rosaire* [Rosary Review], which published a special issue on the canonization of St. Martin de Porres, that took place in Rome on Sunday, 6 May 1962, in the presence of numerous Cooperator Brothers from around the world. Thirty-one Cooperator Brothers from France assembled in Rome with Friar Dominique Frémin for this ceremony.

This text, forty-three years later, has lost none of its freshness, which is why I have set it as Preface for this book. For reasons of health, Friar Dominique Frémin, a member of St. Lazarus convent in Marseille, withdrew to the Hospitaler Brothers of St. John of God in Marseille. In this religious house, he is attended on and finds companionship as well as all the medical services that his state of health requires.

Preface

Current interest in St. Martin de Porres

After three and a half centuries, the figure of St. Martin de Porres surprisingly stirs current interest. This is why the Church presents him to us today as a model to follow. His canonization, in particular, ought to hasten the evangelization of Latin America about which the Holy Father is greatly preoccupied at this moment.

In the world-wide press, there has been much said lately about his influence on the social structures whose development he continues to foster. Is St. Martin not the glory of Peru as well as of all South America? One marvels at his miracles and at the extraordinary gifts with which he was endowed. Even so, Brother Martin would be simply a strange and legendary person in the eyes of our contemporaries if they did not discover at the same time the religious who in all humility consecrated his entire life in the service of God and of others in the Order of St. Dominic.

The Face of Charity: A Man Who Is Aware of His Task

What strikes us the most in the life of St. Martin de Porres is the unlimited charity that urges him on. Even in his lifetime, was he not called "Brother Martin of Charity"? Within the convent as well as outside, he was humbly at the service of others, especially the poor and the outcasts. Not only did he help and support them by innumerable miracles but he taught them genuine technical competencies: those he himself acquired with much eagerness and ability during his apprenticeship with the barber-surgeon. This skill facilitated Brother Martin's charity in favor of the poor and of the sick and allowed him to excel in this work of mercy and compassion simply because he was competent to care for them. In addition, by his reputation and goodness, he was able to garner much cooperation and win the hearts of those whom he would enlist in his mission.

The Face of Charity: A Man of Prayer and Of Penance

In addition, St. Martin de Porres brought about genuine marvels in the domain of charity because he was a man of prayer. Without sparing either strength or time, every day he devoted seven hours to prayer, over and above the long hours spent at the bedside of those who called for him. Kneeling at the foot of the crucifix, he contemplated Christ who gave his life for us and accepted the supreme humiliation of the sacrifice of the Cross. At that time, Brother Martin imposed terrible corporal mortifications on himself, asking God, as did St. Dominic, not to abandon sinners.

His devotion to the Blessed Mother, very simple and heart-felt, was this not like the one of our Blessed Father? During his movements every day, he would thumb his rosary, repeating incessant *Aves* to obtain the help of the Mother of heaven. In prayer at the feet of Our Lady of the Rosary, he entrusted to her the multiple intentions of all those who commended themselves to him.

If the Dominican Cooperator Brother does not have the mission to announce directly the word of God to men, nonetheless, he has as much responsibility as the priest religious in his ministry. The prayer of the Cooperator Brothers is an essential participation in the ministry of their priest-brothers. Besides, by the witness of their life of prayer, the brothers remind men not to rely solely on their energy and human abilities. The brothers are there to signify the apostolic worth of contemplation in a century when only action seems to be efficacious.

The Religious

Obedient, chaste, and poor, Brother Martin lived an exemplary religious life. In all circumstances, he displayed faithful obedience to the orders of his superiors. If he was caught in a failure, it was because charity commanded him to go beyond an order; in certain cases, superiors took this into account, without blaming him.

Brother Martin accepted without complaining all humiliations, even the most cruel. He often sought them out in order to combat pride and remove from his life all vainglory.

He owned nothing personal. Always dressed in used clothing, he shared what was given to him with others, poorer than he. One day, when the convent was indebted, the Prior went to market in order to arrange the sale of some valuable object. Brother ran after him. "I belong to the Order," said he, "sell me! I am almost useless to you." Since this was not his view, the Prior sent Martin back to the convent.

In the common life, Martin was a brother in the background but one with foresight and attentiveness to the needs of everyone. He had deep affection for his brothers. In particular, we see him bound in friendship with Blessed Juan (John) Macias, another cooperator brother of the convent of St. Mary Magdalene in Lima, a man sixteen years younger, who already followed the example of his elder and walked with him on the road to sanctity.

An Appeal for Our Time

Even today. The life of Martin de Porres has been offered to us as a model of religious life. Like him, and following in his footsteps, we are invited to live the Gospel intensively, and bring to men the message of Christ the Savior. No one doubts that St. Martin de Porres will again awaken new vocations and attract men who wish to place themselves in the service of Christ, in this path of noble charity and humility that he himself traveled throughout his life.

Frater Dominique Frémin
Toulouse, 25 March 1962

Introduction

- "Friendship has converted more people than zeal, knowledge or eloquence.
- Sanctity increases very quickly where there is friendship!
- Our world is in desperate search of kindness and friendship."

The roads to sanctity proposed to us throughout the lives of Sts. Martin de Porres and John Macias retrace the way and the life of religious, as modest as they were misunderstood, in the Order of Friars Preachers, otherwise known as "Dominicans."

Their witness confirms us in this shared appeal. Everyone of us is called to holiness; it is even a duty for us. Holiness marks the forehead of the elect. On the day of our baptism, God chose us to be and to become living witnesses of his goodness, his friendship, his love and his glory.

Every Sunday, at Mass, we proclaim in the *Credo*: "I believe in the Church... holy." But, *the Church is us, and we are the church*, as more than a million Haitians sang when they greeted Pope John Paul II who came to visit them. We are therefore *saints*. But we are also sinners. Saints and sinners, this is what we could label our Christian condition, very difficult to live, sometimes, because while it is very evident that we are sinners, we need all our faith to believe that we are saints. And yet, St. Paul calls us "saints." At least thirty times in his Letters, he uses this designation for his recipients. For example, to quote only the Epistle to the Colossians:

Paul, apostle of Christ Jesus... to the saints at Colossae, faithful brothers in Christ. (*Col* 1:2) We have learned of the charity which you have towards all the saints... (*Col* 1:4) God has entrusted me with this mystery . . . that now, has just been manifested to his saints... (*Col* 1:26). You, therefore, chosen by God, his saints and his beloved... (*Col* 3:12)

Holiness Is Our Shared Vocation

It was, first of all the God of Israel who gave us the commandment: "You shall be holy; for I the Lord your God am holy " (*Lv* 19:2). St. Paul reminds us of this requirement when he says: The Father has chosen us in Christ before the foundation of the world that we should be holy an blameless before him. (See: *Eph* 1:4). The Vatican II Council warned us solemnly that the Church is a holy people to the degree that she participates in the triple function of Christ: *sacerdotal, prophetic, and royal* (*Lumen Gentium*, #12). But this holiness of "service" would be nothing without the perfection of charity, which is not optional. Whatever our state in life: married, single, priest, religious ordained or not, we are all called to holiness in Christ. Our calling as Christians is holiness; there is no other response. It is a calling that has its roots in baptism and is proposed anew by the other sacraments, especially in the Eucharist. We are called to holiness at each season of our life: in the springtime of adolescence, in full summer of ripe age, and equally in the autumn and winter of old age, at the hour of death and even beyond death, at the time of the final purification, prepared by the merciful love of God who is infinite and larger than our heart, as the Apostle St. John reminds us.

Becoming a saint is therefore simultaneously an unsullied gift, an acceptance of this voluntary gift, endlessly repeated by God, and a genuine response on our part to trust and follow his will.

The most beautiful gift we received from our parents is the life that develops harmoniously with love and in love. The wonderful heritage that we receive is it not that divine life, that germ of holiness planted in our heart and in our life by the sacrament of baptism? This grace, this gift implants us fully within the Church whose every member reminds us that "God is love." I think of that 16-year-old, Pierre-Yves, who, during a lesson I was giving at the College of Saint-Pierre de Casseneuil, told me: "It's extraordinary: a religion that asks only one thing, to love. He is marvelous, that Jesus, for giving us a single commandment." After a moment of silence, he gazed at me and asked: "Brother, do you yourself practice that commandment of Jesus?"

I replied: "I try." Every one of us entertains the secret thought that one day he will truly conduct his life based on love. It is perhaps urgent to establish and to find again that religion of love in our heart, in those diverse human communities, both Christian and religious. Does not love remain the rock upon which all holiness is built?

The life that I present to you of those two Dominican brothers, acknowledged as saints by the Church, Martin de Porres and John Macias, challenges us to a mission of service so that the Good News be made known to everyone, but especially to the poor.

Good News for the Poor

This statement of Jesus of Nazareth, "Good News for the poor!", is to be taken seriously. The poor, all the poor, await some good news. Often, waiting is all they do: waiting for a roof over their head, something to eat, clothing, a friend, a letter, a visit. They wait to the end of hope, until there is nothing to wait for, until they forget they are waiting.

Moreover, before any misleading spiritual reading, it is in concrete poverty that we appropriately confront our lives: poverty is the lack of the necessary, and the necessary are: food, drink, shelter, clothing, sleep, peace of body and of heart, friendship shared and given, with hand extended. Freedom also, no doubt, since Jesus came to free captives from their chains.

Indeed, there is Good News for the poor. But what is it, and who wishes to announce it to them? Maurice Bellet calls it "divine kindness." Michel de Certeau condenses it in a formula: "not without you." The good and happy news is that everyone of us, absolutely everyone, is necessary for the progress of the world in the eyes of God. But this cannot be uttered, announced, lived, other than through our hands. In truth, it is up to each one to recognize in his surroundings the one to whom he will say: not without you. "I cannot live while ignoring you, I need you to live." And if this is lived in truth, it is truly a question of the kindness of God in this world, of divine kindness, of the friendship of God that is expressed by our smile, our presence, our listening, our patience, our fidelity.

Escorted by You

Since 1990, I have accompanied and traveled with HIV persons or ill with AIDS. According to the dictionary, "accompany" means: *to join a person in order to go where he goes, while at the same time escorting him.*

The accompanying remains, in fact, that section of the trip during which one plumbs the deepest dimension, the most secret of the person, to his basic desire which can be expressed in many ways. Some constants do remain in the diverse forms of accompanying as practiced in our days, because there is always in the person being escorted a precise request for help that is the admission of a need.

What is the one accompanied expecting? The expectations differ from one person to another, or according to age. They range from the need to be aware of a presence, to be heard without being judged, to be recognized, to be appreciated for who one is, all the way to a desire to feel the compassion of another for self — indeed, every one of us needs, more or less, to be pitied.

The needs of people are therefore marked by the idea they have of the role of the one who accompanies. They expect of him sympathy, comfort, a message of hope, relief from culpability. Perhaps they even expect, in the case of a spiritual accompanying, a period of sharing, of listening, and of prayer.

To escort is to enter into a person's present situation, to respect the level of communication being proposed, to refrain from indiscrete questions, and to allow also, if the person has been hurt in his hopes or in his vital powers, the expression of his aggression or his anger.

Spiritual accompanying sustains the person regarding serious existential questions that the trial of sickness or of life continue to present, at one moment or another, especially in the search for internal wholeness and in that legitimate need to be understood, accepted, loved, recognized, esteemed, and appreciated. This also helps the person to find an answer to the meaning of life and to its difficult moments that need to be surpassed.

At the end of life, accompanying makes easier the approach of the passage to death, to the unknown that it represents, and that is often terrifying. It surely allows room for serenity so that the person is able to recover peace within himself, with others, and with life.

It is unbelievable, but when a person is thoroughly escorted, even in his spiritual aspect, I believe that he wishes to live fully up to the end of his life. He completes some projects, adjusts others, progresses in thought, and benefits from life up to the end. I call this course: *to settle accounts at life's end*. Perhaps we can start in daily matters even now, without waiting for the final moments.

Brother Martin de Porres, just like Brother John Macias engaged in this accompanying with persons in need who came to seek from him material and sometimes spiritual help, at the entryway of the convent of Lima. All these individuals wounded by life address them to obtain attentive listening as much as concrete signs and actions of sharing and of love — all these sick individuals whom they took time to visit, to care for, and even to heal, so as to honor the Gospel of compassion to which the Apostle Matthew committed these words of eternal life in his Gospel: In truth, I tell you, to the degree that you have done this for one of the least of my brothers, it was to me that you did it. [See *Mt* 25:31 to 46.]

I am convinced that if they were living in our century, both would have worked actively in the struggle against AIDS and paid attention to the individuals wounded by this lethal virus, who are often rejected, despised, and isolated, and who live in deep loneliness.

In Service to Compassion

Very much like St. Dominic, Martin was fascinated and attracted by what he learned gazing on the cross of Christ, in contemplating the Crucified, as historians affirm. And yet, note well that Brother Martin did not make of the cross a mournful or sickly sweet reading. When I say "reading," I do not exaggerate because he, as much as his brothers, speaks of it as a book to be read. It is for readers the book of charity, the book on the art of loving, the book of life wherein God calls himself love and gives himself in his excessive love for men by means of the life of his Son, Jesus.

The cross of Jesus is the final issue of his life. His death is the price he had to pay to be faithful to the mission with which God had entrusted him: the mission of being witness to the mercy, to the compassion of God that excludes no one, the mission of announcing and setting up the Kingdom of God, a Kingdom of justice, of freedom, and of peace for all mankind.

These words confirm our universal calling as Friars Preachers, ordained or not. It is in this way that I justify the title of this book: *St. Martin de Porres, In service to compassion.*

To fulfill this mission, Jesus gave himself completely, of which his freely accepted death is the ultimate expression. Jesus gave himself out of love, to witness the love of God. Jesus loved up to death! That is why the cross of Jesus becomes a source of life for us. This is why

Brother Martin de Porres placed it in the center of his Dominican religious life, and why his heart overflowed with love and compassion for his neighbor. Compassion is part of our mission, part of the gift of St. Dominic "to lead sinners, the oppressed, and the disheartened into the intimate sanctuary of his compassion." The God of Dominic as much as the God of Martin de Porres is a God of mercy. Compassion presupposes that we abandon the hardness of heart which judges others, that we remove the shell that keeps us apart from others, that we learn to be sensitive to the sufferings and the confusion of others, that we hear their calls for help. This is something we learn in all our communities. Would we dare to let ourselves be touched by the sufferings of our brother in the next room? In case of the opposite, how would we be able to embody the compassion of Dominic, of Martin from Lima and John Macias for the world?

Compassion is more than just a feeling, it is "to open our eyes to see Christ among us." Christ still is suffering, as proved by Las Casas who saw Christ crucified in the Natives of Hispaniola. An education of the heart and of the eye remains necessary to make us attentive to the Lord among us in the oppressed and the wounded. Compassion, therefore, is genuinely contemplative, far-seeing. As Borgman said: "To be touched, moved, by what is happening to people and by what affects them, this is a way of perceiving the presence of God. Compassion is contemplative, in the Dominican meaning." (See: *Letter to our brothers and sisters in initial formation*, 1999, by Timothy Radcliffe.)

Contemplative compassion is the apprenticeship of an unbiased look on others. As such, it remains deeply bound to the thirst of a just world. The involvement of the Order in service to justice and peace becomes easily a question of ideology if it does not arise from contemplative compassion.

A society that does not understand compassion will not understand justice because it will have forgotten the essential: how to understand the other in an unbiased way. It risks seeking refuge in the generalities of prejudices, in deceptive stereotypes.

Practical Guide for the Reader

♦ In order to allow an easy and agreeable reading, the **first chapter** is divided into seven sections, each of which represents a particular aspect of the admirable life of this Dominican Cooperator Brother from Peru. A prayer to St. Martin ends each part, to invite us to meditate on the reading, to enter into prayer, and even to follow a spiritual path in the form of a retreat with this saint, who has been proposed to us as witness for our Christian life.

◆ The **second chapter** recalls the death and the recognition by the entire Church of the holiness of Brother Martin de Porres. It is useful to remember that it was good Pope [now Saint] John XXIII who, at the beginning of Vatican Council II, canonized the first Dominican religious not ordained. This event had been awaited by the entire Church of Peru, which for a long time had honored Brother Martin as her protector for the entire country and a model to imitate, especially for service among people in need, the poor, the sick, strangers, all poorly-loved persons who came to meet him at the door of the convent of Lima.

The holy religious lived the spirit of the Beatitudes that he put into the day-to-day practice of his religious life, by consoling those who were sad, by comforting, visiting, and caring for the sick, by receiving all those who came to the convent requesting a hearing, help, support, words of hope and of life, to renew the courage, respect and dignity of all those who thirsted for justice, peace, and love.

Brother Martin de Porres did not leave us a testament of spiritual writings. The sources for diffusion of his life come from the archives of the Order of Preachers, from a collection of lives of the brethren, and a book by Norbert Georges (a Dominican of the Province of St. Joseph, USA).

◆ **Chapter three** presents three Cooperator Brothers, among the best known and the most illustrious: Bl. Simon Ballachi, Bl. James of Ulm, and St. John Macias, who also lived in Lima as contemporary of Brother Martin. We could have pointed out all the artistic-workers reported in history, thanks to their works of art, and all others, the greater number, who in time remained anonymous in obscurity. All of them led a life of service, hidden and discreet in humility and simplicity.

◆ As **Supplement** is a short historical note recalls that, since the foundation of the Order with St. Dominic, Lay Brothers were present, known as "Cooperator Brothers" since Vatican Council II. Some

Cooperator Brothers speak to present this special, unfamiliar, and thereby underestimated calling.

The announcement of the Gospel of Life invites and urges us to bear witness by our actions more than by our words by becoming good Samaritans of love to our neighbors and especially for persons attained by AIDS with the related association *SELF* (in French: SIDA, Espérance, Lumière, et Foi, i.e., AIDS, Hope, Light, and Faith).

CHAPTER ONE

The Life of St. Martin de Porres (9 Dec 1579 - 3 Nov 1639). Servant of All the Poor: Martin of the Compassion

If there is among you a poor man, one of your brethren in any of the towns within your land which the Lord your God gives you, you shall not harden your heart or close your hand against your poor brother, but you shall open your hand to him and acquiesce to his need, whatever it may be. [See *Dt* 15:7-8.]

1. Birth and Childhood of Martin

Martin de Porres was born in Lima on 9 December 1579 in a modest dwelling facing the Hospital of the Holy Spirit. The municipal council of that city officially authenticated the place of his birth, today transformed into a chapel and enclosed in an enormous apartment building. In November 1939, elaborate ceremonies celebrated the third centenary of the death of the blessed. On that occasion, civil authorities had a plaque mounted in the room where he saw the light of day.

Martin's father, the Spaniard Don Juan de Porres, was a knight of the Order of Alcantara. His mother, Anna Veslasquez, originally from Panama, was a free Black. Their union was not recognized by the Church and they separated after the birth of Juana, their second child.

In the church of St. Sebastian, the font wherein Martin received the sacrament of baptism, on Wednesday, 9 December 1579, as did St. Rose [of Lima] seven years later, still remains there. Consultation of the parochial register attests to the authenticity of the facts. From the fact that their mother belonged to an inferior caste, Don Juan did not wish to acknowledge his children, physically marked by this origin. His dignity was offended by seeing in them the traits of the woman he had seduced. Impelled by pride, humiliated to the quick, he repressed the voice of feelings and of paternal duty. Out of haughtiness, he abandoned his children, objects of humiliation for his pride. In shameful recklessness, he left them with their mother.

From Martin's early infancy, certain indications revealed the holiness to come: admirable humility, uncommon charity toward the poor; as he was growing up, love for the neighbor, especially the sick and the suffering, was developing in his heart. He entertained a special liking for the outcasts. By chance, in the errands given him, he often met some poor unfortunates, more miserable than he. Touched by compassion, the young man gave away the money his mother had entrusted to him. She was greatly vexed at this behavior. Under the circumstances, we can hardly blame her for not recognizing the budding holiness of her child, attested to by his exemplary conduct. She gave him more than one boxing of the ears, something that in no way resulted in a change of his behavior. Grieved for having vexed his mother, Martin willingly accepted the correction; for all that, the satisfaction and the joy of having helped some poor people softened the strictness of the punishment.

Martin was to live and spend his childhood under very humble as well as under very difficult conditions. In certain cases, such a situation could be a handicap and exercise an inauspicious influence on the harmonious development needed for the education of children, which thereby allows them to attain a balanced character. These crises, on the contrary, helped Martin in his advance along supernatural paths. He made himself closer to God. Helped by grace, he developed in the very midst of the disorders of Lima the remarkable piety, the profound understanding of human suffering, that would direct and imbue all his future life and his vocation.

The City of Lima

Lima was a city of sharp contrasts. Like all frontier cities, it counted some depraved persons and some adventurers, the ones overflowing with ill-gotten gains, the others showing themselves greedy for riches and eager for power. But is also included men of state, attorneys, agents to maintain order, and in addition, its saints. It subdued Blacks and Natives, and under pretext of political freedom, was brazenly unjust in paying them laughable wages.

It included slums of distress and of vice, its hovels of physical and moral misery, but is also had homes of virtue, its apostles of charity, its witnesses to compassion and to sanctity that neutralized harmful influences and relieved unfortunate and poor people.

Chapter One

Three saints of Lima figure among the contemporaries of Martin de Porres: the Archbishop Saint Toribio, the Franciscan St. Francis Solano, and Saint Rose, a tertiary of the Order of St. Dominic. [See Chapter 4 for the definition of Dominican tertiary.] Moreover, this city could praise itself for having among its citizens Blessed John Macias, another lay- brother of great merit [See Chapter 3 for cooperator brothers], the Franciscan Fray Juan Gomez, Father Pedro de Urraca, of the Fathers of Mercy, Jesuits such as Father Diego Alvarez de Paz, and Venerable Sebastian de la Parra; and finally, Doña Louisa Melgarejo, of illustrious birth, friend and confidant of Saint Rose.

This list, admittedly incomplete, proves that religion in Lima was something more than pure formalism. It shows that its convents, its magnificent churches, were as many marks that expressed adequately the spirit that animated colonial life in Martin's time. In its religious fervor as much as in its obstruction of law, Lima did not look down on the fine arts, nor the works of the mind. Even before 1600, it had given poetry a significant name, that of the Dominican Ojeda. Statues, paintings, carved objects of gold and silver, still presented today for our admiration, attest to the enthusiasm with which the colonists of the period endeavored to introduce European culture into their new country. Around 1551, less than 15 years after its foundation, Lima sought a royal charter for the University that it was to open in 1553 in the Dominican convent of the Holy Rosary. In spite of its defects and its disorders, Lima, already flourishing in the XVIth century, could rightly boast of being the "City of Kings" and the "Pearl of the Spanish Dominion."

It was in that city of sinners and of saints that the human and spiritual life of Martin developed, in association with an abandoned mother, of modest and shabby status, living in extreme poverty; but who, under the influence of her son, was to free herself from her life of sin and stir up the respect of those who knew her.

Martin was eight years old. His father occasionally came to Lima, but no longer looked at him with as much indifference. In fact, in the city the small half-caste was the object of inexhaustible praise. He was seen as different from other boys, and the father was not unfeeling about this. Even the Spaniards who lived in the neighborhood of Anna Velasquez experienced admiration for that child, whose abandonment heaped blame on the cruel father. But Don Juan did not always ignore the entreaties of a conscience that he had never lost.

Under the influence of his colleagues, won over by the enthusiasm and generosity of Martin, and roused by a sense of duty, Don Juan resolved to recognize his children and took them to Santiago de Guayaquil, where he occupied a post in the name of the King of Spain. There, he entrusted them to a tutor who was to give them rudimentary instruction. Two years later, the Service to the King called Don Juan to Panama. Preferring not to take his children with him, he left the little girl Juana in his Santiago with his uncle, and brought Martin to his mother, who lived in Lima with a middle-class Spanish family.

Martin's Apprenticeship

Anna did her best to complete the education of her son. As soon as he reached his twelfth year, she placed him in apprenticeship with a surgeon. What happiness for Martin; he would be initiated into an attractive profession, exercised all too often by illiterate and unscrupulous barbers. As for Martin, he fulfilled his task conscientiously and with conviction. No doubt, later he would be able to practice charity with greater competence than a surgeon-barber or a phlebotomist. He would seek to discover through all means necessary the therapeutic properties of plants, introduce himself in the art of nursing many afflicted bodies, extract painful decayed teeth, engage in removing malignant growths, study the benefits of balms and ointments, the skill of treating hemorrhages, and especially, he would pray for the sick. God would spare him, no doubt, from the need to earn his support without losing precious time, so precious that it had to be devoted only to prayer and to charitable works in favor of the neighbor in need.

From that time onward, in hospitals, private homes, or in his own home, he filled his days with taking preliminary steps upon himself, in addition, reserving for God, in favor of silence and intimacy, some hours of devotion, properly so-called, that he withheld from sleep. Swallowed up in prayer, he stayed up very late; his spiritual reading required using so many candles, that the proprietor could not contain his curiosity. One night, as he peered through the keyhole of the door, he wanted to investigate what Martin could be doing at such an hour. He saw Martin kneeling before a religious picture, emitting frequent sighs. Suddenly, the latter lifted up his head; you could say that tears bathed his face.

CHAPTER ONE

Martin, the Angel of Kindness for Hospitals and Prisons

From day to day, the reputation of Martin spread throughout the metropolis. An outpouring of esteem attended his untiring enthusiasm, his gentleness and his goodness. His kindness continued to transform and to change more persons than zeal, knowledge, or eloquence. Holiness grows very fast where kindness is shown. Our world is desperately in search of gentleness and kindness, as in this XVIth century in Lima, at the time of Brother Martin. Psalm 86:15 reminds us in prayer: our God is a God of kindness and mercy, full of love and of truth.

Everywhere, Martin met smiling faces. He was the apprentice surgeon, fully in favor of everyone, never escaping from a service to be given, sharing what he had with the poor. He was called: *the angel of hospitals and of prisons.* Obliged to listen to praise and to receive marks of esteem, Martin — very humble of heart and careful not to seek pride in anything — counterbalanced this praise by the mortifications he inflicted on himself in silence and in privacy. This predestined child ceaselessly devoted himself during adolescence to give good example to others, preferring always to do good, filled with modesty, animated by an ardent love for human suffering, thus opening the way to the great works of apostolic charity that God destined for him. In this way, we discover all those dispositions, natural and supernatural, that awakened Martin and opened his heart to genuine compassion.

The good seed sown by Providence had found favorable ground in that young heart as generous as it was enthusiastic, suitable to correspond with grace. Accordingly, it was from the action of this gift that in the heart of his deprivation, Martin learned to place blind confidence in the Savior of men: Jesus Christ.

Prayer to St. Martin de Porres

1. *God Directs Us*

O blessed Martin, not content with being the son of a Black, you allowed yourself to be directed in your childhood by the hand of God, obtain for us to accept always the designs of Providence.

By following your example, support us in recognizing the will of the Lord even in our trials. You have taught us that if we are upright and generous with him, he will be merciful and compassionate towards us. We wish to follow him faithfully.

Help us and pray for us to your beloved Jesus, the Son of God, who with the Father and the Holy Spirit, lives and reigns for ever.

Amen.

CHAPTER ONE

2. The Vocation of Martin: In the Footsteps of St. Dominic

For a long time, Martin wished to give his life totally to the service of the Lord. The call to religious life seemed decisive for him. He opted for the Order of Friars Preachers. Often, he had been seen absorbed in prayer before the Blessed Sacrament in their attractive church of the Holy Rosary. Martin came to understand that for the children of St. Dominic the preaching of the Word of God was put into concrete form in works of mercy and compassion and had their source, as did their influence, in diligent contemplation and in regular appointments with silent prayer. Accordingly, he went to knock at the door of the convent of the Holy Rosary and requested his admission. In humility, he did not ask for the habit of the regular lay brother of the First Order; that would have been too superior for him. He simply intended to offer himself to the service of the convent as a tertiary or a coadjutor. Father Juan de Lorenzana, Provincial of Peru, had received details about the exceptional gifts and the exemplary life of Martin. Don Juan, without opposing the calling of his son, would have preferred to see him clothed with the habit of the regular lay Brother. But Martin's decision was pressing: he wished to occupy the lowest place, to be closer to God, the better to serve him in this manner.

At age fifteen, Martin received the holy habit of Dominican tertiary: white tunic, black scapular and cappa. Nine years later, his superiors ordered him, in virtue of holy obedience, to pronounce solemn vows that placed him in the ranks of the regular lay Brothers of the First Order of St. Dominic.

Brother Martin was appointed to various convent duties: barber, infirmarian, keeper of the clothes closet. Frugal towards himself in favor of benefit to everyone, he served the other promptly and scrupulously, with discretion and care, thinking of everything for everyone, always attentive to the presence of God within himself. To his patience as infirmarian, he added an indispensable yet persuasive firmness. The welcome he reserved for the wishes of the brothers or sick individuals, did not lead him to acquiesce blindly to their whims. He surrounded them with angelic affection, comforted them in hours of discouragement, and waited on them while kneeling.

His preference inclined him to accept the most humble duties. One day, a religious seeing him pass by the washroom, busy with lowly tasks, told him humorously: "Now, Brother Martin... you would be better at the archiespiscopal palace of Mexico than here. Don't you think?" The saint retorted with a mischievous quote from Psalm 84: "I have chosen to be lowly in the house of my God, rather than to live in the tent of sinners." [See *Ps* 84:10.] This was not a criticism of the Archbishop's residence ,who during his passage through Lima some time earlier, had asked for the services of Brother Martin. The latter simply wanted to indicate that with the unnatural ceremony that enveloped the bigwigs of the world, he preferred pleasing discretion and humility.

Truth be told, the Archbishop in question, Msgr. Feliciano de Voga, held him in high esteem. A cleric, knowing this and anxious to obtain sacred orders, addressed the humble religious: "Dear Brother Martin, who you have much influence with the Archbishop and on his councillors, would you not plead my cause?" "Come, dear friend," replied Martin. "How can you add so much credence to those rumors. Those pretended honors, those marks of esteem of which I am the object, even on the part of the Archbishop, do you take them seriously?"

Martin pushed self-denial and self-effacement to their limits. The convent had a debt to pay and creditors so pressed their demands that the Prior, in desperation, had to sell some valuables to the best buyer on the market. Barely arrived at the place, he saw Brother Martin, running, out of breath... "Father," said he, puffing, "I know you have a debt to pay. But, thank Heaven, we have the means to discharge it. I am but a poor mulatto. I belong to the Order, and it has always treated me with kindness, accordingly, I am, so to speak, useless. Sell me. Grant me this favor, I pray you. Perhaps someone will be able to make me work as I should."

Amused and touched at the same time, the Prior gently ordered him to return to the convent.

Martin never had the idea of resting in his room; he never had time. At night, the task of infirmarian often kept him at the beside of a sick individual or of a religious. If he had need of a bit of sleep, he used to stretch out in the chapter hall, on the pallet used to transport the dead. This is how he gave his tired body a minimum of rest. One winter, struck with fever and completely indifferent to the care needed for his state, he grew so weak that certain religious, alarmed, informed the Prior. The latter wanted Martin to get a bed for himself, with mattress, sheets and blankets. The sick man obeyed immediately. When the religious who remained alert, noticed that he slept fully dressed with shoes on his feet, they accused him of disobedience before the Prior. He replied discretely to their concern. "Brother Martin is a capable mystical theologian. His theology has taught him he secret of uniting obedience to mortification."

Truly, Brother Martin had a horror of sleeping in a comfortable bed! The Provincial himself had to intervene to have him sleep like all the Brothers. The retort by Brother Martin, just as we have preserved it, was rather direct: "What? Your Reverence orders someone who has never known in his home the refinement of comfort to prepare for himself a downy bed? My Father, I pray you: do not compel me to such a luxury." Nonetheless, that night he had to slip in between the sheets. Only, so as not to experience well-being, he kept on his coarse hair shirt and his woolen tunic. Father Provincial, Louis de Bilbao, was informed and objected to him: "Brother Martin, is this how you obey me" ... "Father," replied Brother Martin, "the relief that I experienced was very sufficient. On using the bed, I obeyed you; on sleeping fully dressed, I treated my body as it deserved."

The Poverty of Brother Martin

Martin de Porres held Holy Poverty in sincere devotion. He wished to have only two patched tunics, falling into pieces. "In the convent ," he stated, "the more the habits are used, the more stylish they are for me. I have two, that's more than enough. It is easy for me to wash the one I am not wearing." He had an inclination for the "old", the "no longer in use." If he could not do otherwise but to accept new shoes, he was quick to lend them to a destitute person for his use after they had become worn. The reason he used to justify this behavior was rather naive: "By wearing old habits and worn shoes, I no longer have to care for them. If I lose them, it is not serious." He gave in to a minor fancy. The Dominicans of the Province of Peru used to wear their rosary around the neck. Martin wore another one at his belt, as is generally done by most of the Brothers of the Order of St. Dominic.

Martin also lived daily in the spirit of the Constitutions, in observance of what the Lord said: Go, sell all you own, give to the poor, and come, follow me. [See *Mt* 19:21.]

We have decided to become poor in fact and in spirit so that, striving to tear men from the domination of riches and to turn them towards the goods from above, we ourselves may become conquerors of avarice by our conformity to Christ who made himself poor for us, so as to enrich us by his poverty. [See *2 Cor*, chaps. 8 & 9.]

Brother Martin's room reflected his spirit of poverty. His furniture consisted of a pallet [a straw bed], on which he stretched out in case of such fatigue that he could not work. Affixed to the wall, a wooden cross, an image of the Holy Virgin, and another of St. Dominic.

Whether in the clothing storeroom, in the infirmary, or during his charitable trips throughout the city, he seemed to be endowed with the gift of ubiquity [being in two places at the same time], to the point of never, in some way, being in the place where he was supposed to be. When he entered his room, it was at night, at the end of his long and tedious days of work, to find a necessary refuge as much for his prayers as for essential rest.

The Raptures of Brother Martin

At the time, the convent was offering hospitality to a young Spaniard, Juan Vasquez, whom Martin had recovered half-dead and employed in the distribution of his alms. One night, when a violent earthquake shook the city, the child awoke with a start and in fear, ran to seek refuge with Brother Martin. After having knocked persistently but in vain, he pushed open the door. Imagine his astonishment to find the Brother in a major prostration, arms outstretched in a cross, rosary in hand. He called and called, and called again, tugging at his garments; but Martin did not budge. Thinking that his protector was dead, the boy fled in fear. The mulatto's room was flooded with light, in the middle of the night, as if it were full daytime.

One day, Juan Vasquez surprised Brother Martin in his room, kneeling in the open, a meter off the floor, arms in a cross, eyes fixed on the crucifix. Trembling with emotion, Juan left in a flash to relate the marvel to the porter, Brother Ferdinand of Aragon. The quiet and smiling answer of the latter only increased the astonishment of the child. "Do not be surprised by the raptures of Martin. This is not the first time. You will get used to them."

One day, another tertiary, Brother Martin Cabezas, was looking for Brother Martin to have him speedily go to Father Anthony d'Arc, who was agonizing. He found the blessed in the chapter hall, in the state of levitation, pressing his lips to the image of his Redeemer, at the site of the wound on his side. Stupefied, the tertiary sped into the cloister, taking with him to the site of the marvel, Fathers Diego Borrionuevo and Stephen Mariano. After a brief moment, the saw the Saint slowly come down, following a supernatural premonition that he was wanted in the infirmary. Brother Martin replied calmly: "Father Anthony has only to prepare carefully for his death. His hour has come."

Martin endeavored to receive the extraordinary favors God granted him. At night time, the solitude of his room, the Chapter Hall, were ordinarily their stage. But sometimes God allowed the presence of witnesses. Thus, one night, during the singing of Matins, a bright light bathed the main altar. The religious then saw Brother Martin in full ecstasy. His face shone with celestial brightness. By this subtle sign, God chose to manifest the satisfaction he received from this humble and happy son of St. Dominic.

Prayer to St. Martin de Porres

2. Vocation

O Glorious Brother Martin, you who have followed the path of the Lord from childhood up to answering the call of your vocation to live and share in the mission of our Father St. Dominic in the Order of Friars Preachers, with always strong faith and confidence in God, filled with zeal for his glory and the salvation of everyone, obtain for us to live in that same faith as the children of God that we are.

Pray for us so that we might imitate your loyalty and be given the special graces which all of us need — you who are able to ask everything from our king, Jesus Christ, who lives and reigns forever.

Amen.

3. Brother to the Poor: Martin of Charity

The beneficial activity of Brother Martin shone well beyond the city. The convent of the Holy Rosary appeared too restricted to allow for the expansion of his charitable zeal. He was not the victim of that collective egoism seeing only close-by brothers needing help. The generosity of his heart was not limited solely to the Dominican Order. The sick, the poor, the afflicted along with sinners, were his favorite companions. Martin scoured the city, healing some, comforting others. He was occasionally sent outside the limits of Lima; his holiness led him to improbable distances.

A public official in Lima, Don Juan de Figuero, friend of the Blessed, had him come one day to treat him for an alarming sore throat. After a brief conversation, the good brother assured him of a cure and excused himself for having to leave so hurriedly. He placed on the table, a flask and left quickly with no other explanation. Stunned, the official took the flask in hand, and had the idea of taking it to his lips. He drank a bit of its contents, and was instantly cured. He understood, then, the abrupt departure of Brother Martin, preoccupied with sparing himself from whatever praise could come from his exercise of miraculous power.

Marveling at the cure of her master, a servant, who had long been suffering from a skin disease that disfigured her, washed her face with the water — indeed, it was only water — contained in the flask and found herself instantly cured.

A poor man had a wound whose infection placed his life in danger. Martin tended to it, made a sign of the cross on an application of rosemary powder. Four days later, the sore was closed. By the sign of the cross, he cured another unfortunate man whose legs were covered with cankers. In sympathy with Elizabeth Orthez de Torrez because of her sufferings, following an intense hemorrhage, he gave her perfect health.

During a charitable mission in the surrounding countryside, the feet of Juan Vasquez were so swollen that Martin, noticing that the boy was unable to get to the convent, cured him without delay.

Juana, the sister of St. Martin de Porres, lived in a suburb of Lima. Victim of an accident, one of her servants was gravely wounded on the face. The blessed made a sign of the cross and the bloodied face recovered automatically its normal appearance.

Chapter One

A novice at the convent of St. Magdalen in Lima, Luis Guttierez, cut two of his fingers with a very sharp knife. The infection menaced the entire hand. Brother Martin was, at that very moment, visiting his friend, Blessed John Macias. Informed, he examined the wound. "Fear not, dear child," said Martin. "The Lord, Master of life and death, will bless the wound, whatever its seriousness." The infirmarian, carrying his inevitable medicine kit, took a bit of powder of Holy Mary herb, cleaned the black and blue fingers and made a fervent sign of the cross. On the following day, the fingers had resumed their habitual form, and their normal agility.

Some Miraculous Cures by Brother Martin

Miracles performed by Brother Martin at the convent of the Holy Rosary are so numerous that we can bring to mind only a few of them.

Struck down by a deadly pleurisy, Father Luis de Guadalupe was preparing his final confession. Brother Martin entered his room. Immediately, the sick man felt a renewal of hope and of comfort. "Set your medicine aside, Brother Martin; place your hand here, at my side..." Such was his suffering! Martin acceded to the dying wish. Immediately, Father Luis felt much better. "God be praised," said he, euphoric and surprised. "I am doing much better and have no need of your medicine." The Blessed had used neither herb nor medicine. The simple contact of the hand produced the healing, for which he felt himself deeply humiliated, Moreover, he left completely embarrassed. "That's a good one... To play such a trick on a poor mulatto!"

Martin was the author of a similar cure for the benefit of a religious of rather difficult character. No doubt, we can understand that Father Pedro de Montesdosca tormented himself for having to undergo the amputation of a leg taken over by gangrene, but why did he take it out on whoever came to comfort him? No one dared to enter his room. Now Brother Martin had a divine inspiration; he realized that the sick man, in the throes of fever and delirium, was longing for one of his favorite meals. Considering the fearful sufferings of the patient, he prepared and served the religious the refreshing salad of which he was dreaming. The reaction was exactly the one expected. The ill-humor of Father Pedro faded away. He suddenly recovered peace of soul and hope in the goodness of God. He asked Brother Martin to place his hand on the gangrenous limb and to pray for him.

Soon, Father Pedro began to walk.

Never would Brother Martin be seen with empty hands: he was always thinking of the poor, of sick persons. Whether in town or in the convent itself, he always kept hidden under his habit: medicine, bread, and fruits. During his course, joy radiated from this giver of benefits, this purveyor of comfort.

His incredible premonition of the needs of others gave him no respite. This is what took him out of his room, sent him out of the convent, to the point of having him leave the city. From a distance, Martin heard the groans of the poor ashamed to beg. And so, he went to these unfortunates secretly, to distribute his gifts and see the light of hope in their eyes, up to then so hopeless. How many times did Martin not help with his generosity toward priests lodged in hovels, and who, for the most part, to ward off embarrassing financial straights were obliged to engage in work unsuitable to their character!

For many months, Brother Martin could be seen, carrying food and clothing, heading every day toward Gallac, eight kilometers from Lima, where he knew that the soldiers garrisoned there lacked strict basics. His decision had been prompt. Yet, the distance was long and painful, through an almost deserted countryside, by steep roads and under a blazing sun. His shoulders felt the weight of the daily load, containing a share for each individual soldier. But no matter!

When Martin had nothing to give, he was skilled in using a particular gift for a purpose different from the one to which a praiseworthy intention had moved him. Here are a few examples.

One day, Brother Martin was walking along the prison of Lima. Some detainees doing hard labor in the courtyard recognized him. The asked him for food and drink. Alas, the good Brother had no more bread. A moment of reflection: how to help these starving individuals?... An idea came to his head. Paying little attention to the blazing sun, he hurried to sell his hat to buy bread for these unfortunates, whose confident request had moved him.

Catalina de Porres, niece of the Blessed, reported that one day, when her uncle presumed her permission to dispose of a large sum that she had placed with a trader, he went to the store followed by a string of poor people and bought shoes and clothes that he distributed to them. Catalina wept bitterly over it. "While my tears were still flowing," she relates, "Martin came to me, saying with his usual luminous smile, not to be sad: the money would be returned to her. In fact, on the following day, the four thousand *reals* were restored to me at the behest of Brother Martin de Porres." We refrain from explaining this manner of misappropriation of funds. Relying on the Providence of God, Martin was convinced that the money, needed more by the poor than by his niece, would be restored to her. Several times, Martin assured his sister and his niece that in their case of need, he would come to help. This indeed happened, in fact many times, in his unpremeditated manner.

It is simply that he saw the suffering Christ in the sick, the poor, the afflicted. One day, he met an old beggar, half naked and covered with sores. He carried him to his room, laid him in his bed, provided him with everything he needed and cared for him tenderly until he was fully cured. Another brother of the convent blamed him sharply, muttering that he should not have placed in his bed so unpleasant a beggar. "Compassion, my dear friend, is preferable to cleanliness. Do not forget," he added, "that is easy enough for me to wash my sheets with a bit of soap, when a torrent of tears could never cleanse the fault committed by hardness of heart toward an unfortunate person."

At every moment, someone was at the convent asking for Brother Martin, either for some bread, for some medicine, or for prayers. He received with equal goodness, Spaniards, Indians, and Blacks. He ministered to them without counting, fed them, lodged them, instructed them in their religious duties. The crowding of hospitals often obliged him to take a poor person into his room or into an unoccupied room. Blessed Martin ended up harboring such a large number of unfortunates that Father Provincial was obliged to intervene. He gave orders to Martin to prevent persons in need from having access to the convent, allowing him, however, the option to care for and receive them in some other location. Martin's sister offered him a house she owned outside the city where he could give asylum to persons rejected or on the margins of society.

The Compassion of Brother Martin

Nonetheless, one night when Martin was returning to the convent, he noticed an Indian victim of an attack. The unfortunate had bled profusely and was close to death.

After hastily placing a bandage, Martin carried him to his nearby convent, placed him in his own bed and did the impossible to save his life, planning to transport him to his sister, as soon as the state of the wounded man allowed. The Provincial, poorly informed, perhaps even on the pretext of testing the humility of the holy man, did not see the situation in the same light. He reprimanded Martin severely for having disobeyed his clear orders: no sick person was to enter the cloister, and this prohibition extended to Brother Martin as well as to the other religious of the community. Accordingly, the Provincial imposed on him a severe punishment for having broken the rule. Martin received it with joy and humility, without uttering a word.

In the meantime, a few days later he was summoned to render service to the Provincial, He knelt humbly before him, requested his blessing, and asked forgiveness for having broken his orders. The Provincial replied: "Brother Martin, I meant simply to punish your disobedience." "Pardon me," said Martin, "but allow me to enlighten you... I was unaware that the precept of obedience superseded that of charity." Driven into a corner by Martin's good sense, the Provincial could not do otherwise than to permit him to continue his works of charity and compassion in the convent of the Holy Rosary.

Brother Martin helped many other sick and persons near death besides those in the convent or in his sister's house. It is difficult for us to understand how he managed to busy himself with all his dependents while at the same time facing the obligations assigned to him, or being sent to Limatambo, two miles from the city, to work at a farm belonging to the convent. When returning at night, he still found a way to visit the sick in the neighborhood. He distributed medicine, dressed their wounds, and brought them back to health. A word, a service, became a ray of sunshine reviving those persons living in fear and hopelessness. When he had an inkling of some feeling of resistance, he tried to calm it by his kind sympathy. Were he to see a Black man on the point of death, Martin immediately called for a priest and used kindness to bring back to God the soul that was about to meet him. After death ensued, he made it a duty to assure a decent burial, often lending a hand in this ultimate act of charity. Martin was a forerunner in this matter.

Did you know that in the year 2000, in Paris, an organization struggled actively for greater dignity of burials of individuals who died in the street, the homeless, and those who have no survivors. Again in Paris and its suburbs, every year more than six hundred twenty persons are buried at Thiais [a potter's field - Trans.]. For those who die alone or anonymously, Thiais is the final stop but also the last leg of a long administrative process. When an individual dies isolated in the street or in a home, only the police have the authority to determine the cause of death. The corpse is then brought to the medico-legal institute where an investigation is held to determine the cause of death and look for eventual heirs. After about one month's delay, if no family member has made himself known, the morgue requests the burial through administrative channels. The corpses are the transported to Thiais by volunteer processions, if the family lacks the means to pay for a funeral or friends ask for one. Bodies rest at Thiais for five years before being exhumed and cremated.

Martin's sincere compassion for human suffering, the warmth of his charity, his understanding of the fatherhood of God and the brotherhood of men, gave to his love for Christ a character of genuineness. All by itself, compassion brings consolation and calm. If mercy falls from the merciful to the miserable, compassion presupposes equality of nature; one sees himself on the same level as the person being put to the test. Better still, the former bears the latter's misfortune with and like him (the meaning of *cum-pati*), as if it were his own. "For a child to be able to cherish his mother, she must have suffered with him, and shared his sorrows." Compassion does more than accompany, it shares, it becomes identified. Only in his way does true love prove itself: a love steeped in sorrow, drinking from the same chalice. Accordingly, we think of Jesus in his solitude and in prayer at the hour of the gift of his life in the Garden of Gethsemani — just as Brother Martin who wished to follow the Son of God on this same path.

To improve the situation for needy persons, Martin followed a very definite plan. His charity was universal; no one fell outside his concern: the living, the dead, men, women, children, priests, lay persons, Spaniards or Peruvians, Indians or Blacks.

Orphans, children abandoned and homeless, were always the objects of his deep compassion. Especially did he consider the dangers to which these unfortunates were exposed. If Catholic schools were not maintained to insure their subsistence and their moral formation, how could anyone expect to make of them honest citizens, sincere Christians? The Blessed pleaded their cause with such enthusiasm and with such persevering conviction that he ended up by obtaining support and subsidies from civil and religious authorities. He was able to interest many wealthy persons who generously helped him to realize his project. It was thanks to his influence that a rich merchant, Matthew Pastor and his wife, Frances Valdez, founded the college and the orphanage of the Holy Cross. Today, these two educational establishments continue this mission and carry the name of their protector, St. Martin de Porres. Only God will ever know what good this institution was able to accomplish in favor of girls, first of all, and then of boys, on the social as well as on the religious level. This is a striking illustration of the power of grace, supporting the efforts of a humble man, unbiased, convinced and enthusiastic, simultaneously governed and guided by a genuine social and Christian consciousness.

Prayer to St. Martin de Porres

3. The Mission of Love

>Glorious St. Martin, always compassionate, brother to the poor and to those in need, look upon us with compassion and pray for us who call upon you with strong faith in your goodness and in your mission of love.
>
>Do not forget us before God whom you always served and adored — Father, Son and Holy Spirit — whom we also wish to serve and adore following your example, now and for all eternity.
>
>Amen.

CHAPTER ONE

4. The Extent of Brother Martin's Charity

In order to exercise his multiform charity, Brother Martin considered time as being among the most precious elements. We admire the diversity of his works of mercy, his cleverness and his untiring enthusiasm, the success of his altruistic activities. To what, then, can we attribute the success of his apostolate among the poor, if not in large part to that spontaneous and total generosity to this or that charitable work, whose urgency he often suddenly realized? The life of Blessed Martin is a total refutation of the current objection of lack of time to excuse a failure in practicing works of mercy. His impartiality was absolute. Never did he allow sparing himself before the possibility of doing good. The misfortune of his neighbor, whatever form it might take, aroused his compassion. To relieve suffering was for him an irresistible need. He never claimed, as we could do, that his multiple duties, an abundance of chores or religious responsibilities, obliged him to set "limits" in the exercise of charity. On the contrary, he eagerly sought all occasions possible to bend to the suffering and to the comfort of unfortunate and afflicted persons. Consequently, his charity was exercised for every objective and without restrictions.

Martin, the "Angel of Peace"

First of all, his own, as is appropriate, were the object of his charity. At one point, misunderstanding threatened to break the conjugal life of his sister Juana, who regularly avoided keeping him informed of the difficulties she was experiencing in her family life. Nonetheless, warned interiorly of the imminence of a break, Martin took to the road. His sister Juanna and her husband lived about a mile away from Lima. The two spouses had engaged in such violent quarrels that neighbors were forced to intervene. The outcome seemed to require a definite separation when Martin appeared at their threshold carrying a basket of bread, wine, and fruits. Immediately both lowered their eyes, became silent, and found their composure. The "Messenger of Peace" laid out in fine detail the difficulties that had caused the dispute, even though neither of them had informed him about them. He went back to the deep and secret causes that pride and self-esteem had arranged to confirm their stands. He unraveled tactfully and opportunely treacherous knots that had impeded their love. After having set them on the path of peace, he reproached them severely for their conduct. The spouses reconciled and accepted this painful lesson with gratitude; from then on, they would know how to love each other while forgetting the self. The neighbors, instructed in turn, left after consuming the wine and the fruit.

Other similar reconciliations won for Martin the nickname "angel of peace." He performed this role by means proper to himself. He communicated his overflowing charity to those who lacked any. From his person, there flowed a heavenly peace. His mission consisted precisely in distributing around him that peace of mind and of heart, arising from perfect obedience to the divine will, an unchangeable peace, to unaware worldly people.

But Martin was a positive angel of peace. He thought of everything that could make the poor as happy as possible, at all levels. On the outskirts of Lima, Brother Martin had long noticed a rather barren hill, but well situated because of its proximity to the city. No one had ever cared to exploit that ungrateful soil. Poor as well as rich dreamed of easier gains. In his moments of leisure, Brother Martin planted some fruit trees that were likely to provide abundant fruit. "Within three years," he thought, "this plantation will be the legacy of the poor. The harvest will be sufficiently abundant to fill their needs, so they will no longer succumb to the temptation of plundering the nearby orchards. This would be a benefit for their soul and protection for the landowners." This mark of foresight specific to him and a picture of him, inviting the boys of Lima to share the fruits of the orchard, bear witness to the generosity of his heart.

The Charity of Brother Martin for Animals

One could be surprised at the interest he had for the least of creatures. This was simply the overflowing of a superabundant zeal without limits. Like St. Francis of Assisi, Martin was convinced that all creatures, however base or despicable they were, filled a role in the plan of creation. Without this attention, the life of Blessed Martin would remain an enigma. Undoubtedly, he had what we could call with Chesterton "an understanding of the divine temperament." Why is it startling that he took care of rats, of mice, of dogs, and of cats? The beauty of his nature explains this for us, and is also witness of a love without limits for all created beings, the manifestation of an exceptional gift that bypassed the laws of space and of time. This beneficence therefore extended to animals. Martin could not conceive that God would have created a living being to become a beast of burden or a plaything of the athlete. He told himself that animals would suffer less evil treatment from man if the latter, endowed with intelligence, realized that it is inhumane and senseless to be cruel towards them. We have numerous proofs of the goodness, the tenderness even of Brother Martin towards our lower brothers. One day, while crossing a street, he spied a dog with a bloody wound. He approached the poor beast. "Poor little one," said he; " you had wanted to be mischievous; you picked a fight.. And what a mess you are now! Come with me; I will try to get you into a better condition." Arrived at the convent, he laid out the dog on a mat, washed his wound and poured some ointment. A few days later, he sent off the healed animal.

Fernando Arragones told of the Procurator of Holy Rosary had ordered the Black employees in the kitchen to kill an old dog, who, for eight years had been his faithful companion. Martin met the men as they were ready to dispose of the body of the beast on top of a heap of rubbish. The blessed, knowing full well that it was not a question of a natural death, had the corpse of the dog taken to his cell, then went looking for the Procurator to protest sharply to him. "It is unbecoming of you to have your old servant and friend disappear in this way. All the services that it rendered you certainly was worth allowing this poor beast to finish its days peacefully." After this reprimand, continued Fernando Arragones, the servant of God returned to his room, brought the dog back to life, and on the following day went to get it some food from the kitchen of the infirmary. He saved it a niche in his room and forbad it to approach its former master. The dog obeyed as if he had been endowed with reason.

Brother Martin noticed that a mule belonging to an Indian had fallen into a deep pit. The beast was making vain efforts to get out. Martin arrived, and addressing the mule in an peremptory tone told him: "Creature of God, get out of there." As if by enchantment, the mule regained the surface.

An enraged bull had escaped and was sowing panic in the streets of the city. Martin was entering the convent when he noticed the confusion of the crowd as it pushed cries of fear. Then, slowly, he approached the bull and with a simple gesture restored its calm.

His goodness extended even to noxious creatures: for a while, the convent of the Holy Rosary was infested with mice and rats; they caused much damage to linens and to clothing, in the sacristy, the clothes closet, the rooms. So much so that the decision was made to exterminate them. Brother Martin was greatly moved to think that these unbearable but innocent little beasts were destined to a merciless punishment. On seeing a small rat, "Little brother rat, listen to me," he told it. "You are no longer safe here. Tell your companions to get together in the shed at the end of the garden." At these words, tradition reports, the messenger went to accomplish his mission to the tribes of rodents. A long line of rats and mice could be seen marching along the cloister to the old shed designated by Brother Martin. This episode earned him the nickname: Pied Piper. We know that, according to the poem of Robert Browning, the first Pied Piper laid a trap for the rats of Hamelin Town: he bewitched them with music and led them to the edge of the river "where all plunged in and were drowned." And, by the way, let it be said that the thousand guilders that he earned were never paid by the mayor. As for Martin, instead of destroying the rats, he worked at preserving their lives, all the while impeding their deleterious behavior.

The Gospel of the Compassion with Brother Martin

An image of the Blessed represents him having cats and dogs next to each other, eating the same food, in perfect understanding; even more, a cat is eating with a mouse. This symbol of Martin's extreme goodness suggests what must have been the sincerity and the depth of his noble heart. The neighbor, whoever he was, shared in the treasures of his noble heart. He fed those who were hungry, provided beverages for those who were thirsty, mitigated pains, relieved distress, enlightened those who found themselves in the dark. He put into practice that passage of the Gospel that we know so well. At the eve of our life, the Lord will say to each one of us: What did you do when I was hungry, thirsty, a stranger, sick, in prison, or naked? [See *Mt* 25:31-46.]

In that teaching, the response of Jesus cannot leave us insensitive: In truth, I tell you; to the degree that you did this for one of the least of my brothers, you did it for me.

To put this in another way, the closest friend of Jesus, the apostle John, transmits it to us in his Gospel: You will be recognized by this sign, the love you have for one another. [See *Jn* 13:35.] Such is the message of Brother Martin who, during his entire life, gave witness to the Gospel of compassion and of love for his neighbor. It is the sign of our universal vocation, as the Rule of St. Augustine reminds us: Before everything, dear brothers, let us love God and love our neighbor; these are the commandments that were first given to us. [See *Mt.* 22:36-40.]

God had chosen him to channel his grace and mercy. Martin's superiors, brothers, friends, the poor, the sick, homeless children, all benefitted from the favors that flowed, as from a spring, from the heart of this mulatto.

And yet, the invisible world was no stranger to him. He had a special devotion to his guardian angel, to St. Dominic and to St. Joseph. In the hall next to the refectory, there stood a statue of the Holy Virgin. Martin was happy to decorate it with flowers and there to burn some candles. He also had a fervent habit of praying the Rosary. Our Lady appeared to him often, carrying the Child Jesus in her arms. She spoke at length with him at night, in the dormitory, in the chapel after matins, where he loved to remain alone to pray.

Prayer to St. Martin de Porres

4. Compassion

> On this earth, O blessed Martin, you lived only for God and for your neighbor. You cherished all the other creatures of God and had the same special and supernatural inclinations toward all animals. Now, seated near the throne of goodness and mercy, you are better able to distribute its treasures. Look favorably, Blessed Martin, on those who come to you in the assurance that they will be heard.
>
> Help us to follow you on the path of compassion so that we may one day know the glory of heaven where you praise God in the company of the angels and the saints for all eternity. Amen.

5. The Mortifications of Brother Martin

Brother Martin was deeply convinced of the need for penance. In the course of his life, he strove earnestly and courageously on all occasions to practice severe mortifications. His brothers in religion, like the inhabitants of the city, were witnesses to his sanctity; but out of humility, he lived in a discreet almost secret manner his spirit of repentance, just as he did for the remarkable favors he received. Perfectly indifferent, he remained a stranger to all ostentation. Never did the thought that he could be a saint cross his mind. His attraction for penance was a mark of his deep love for Christ the Redeemer and a means of converting himself so as to respond to Jesus's love.

And yet, Father Gaspard de Soldagna, Prior of the convent, felt it his duty to leave posterity an example: that of the mortifications the religious attempted to hide. For this purpose, he ordered Martin to compile a report of all his daily penitential practices. Was it true that our Father St. Dominic inflicted the discipline [a whip - Trans.] on himself three times a night? For Martin to answer this request was painful. Confused, he hesitated for a moment, but then, out of obedience answered: "Good Father, God will make this known when it pleases him. Yes, I will confess simply that I give myself the discipline three times a night, following the example of our glorious Father and Founder." Then, he entreated the Superior to put an end to this painful questioning, a favor that the latter kindly granted.

Biographies of the Blessed report that his penances were spontaneous, rigorous, and steady. He practiced them in all spheres. A penitent even before entering the Order, he remained one up to his death. But Martin took care to keep hidden from the eyes of men his startling austerities. What the world saw was his manner of glorifying God, of comforting and healing afflicted persons. In his eyes, suffering was a ransom for love, albeit an insufficient ransom. One of his friends asked him why he punished his body mercilessly. Martin answered simply: "My salvation requires this strictness and my faults deserve even more."

Martin de Porres ate barely enough to avoid fainting away. Like the sons of St. Dominic, he observed abstinence and continual fasts. During Lent, he ate a bit of bread and some water. From Holy Thursday to Easter Sunday, at noon, he ate absolutely nothing. On Sundays and feast days of the Church and of the Order when it was permissible to rejoice, he ate vegetables, greens, or those tasteless and poorly nutritious roots that the Peruvians called *yuccas* [a flowering plant of many uses - Trans.]. Despite this frugal nourishment, Martin was able to provide the work of many common laborers.

The Whippings of Brother Martin

Only to his Superior did Brother Martin reveal the number of his whippings, but there were witnesses, able to speak of them. God allowed the holiness of his servant to be an object of edification for posterity. The discipline that Brother Martin used was not a simple rope with knots but rather a chain with hooks of metal. When blood flowed over his shoulders, he rubbed them with salt and vinegar, hoping with this increase of suffering to obtain the conversion of sinners and atone for his personal faults.

After the first nightly whipping, he went to the chapter room where, before the crucifix, he meditated on the Passion of the Savior and prepared for the second whipping by prayer that enlivened his fervor. He would remove the undershirt which adhered to his wounds, thereby renewing the previous sufferings. He treated his body with heightened rigor as much for the conversion of sinners as for their return to the Lord. After having meditated on the unspeakable sufferings of the Passion, what did he care for the blood flowing onto his floor? The salvation of sinners was worth all the sufferings he inflicted on himself; this essential concern explains for us his extreme severity on this point.

Worn out from this second whipping, the holy Brother agreed to take a bit of rest, laying down on a stretcher used to transport the dead, or else he went to sit down in the infirmary where he slept until dawn. Then, prompt and silently, he went down to an underground room where one of his most severe tortures awaited him.

At dawn, in fact, a young man, faithful to the dreadful daily meeting, awaited him. He was a native, stalwart and pitiless, an Inca devoted and faithful, that the blessed had deliberately chosen. For the third time, with no consideration for the wounds to his undershirt from the sleep, but with a quick move, he bared his back, giving the signal for the whipping to begin. Armed with a branch of the wild quince tree, the tormentor struck with unflagging energy, application, and enthusiasm, stimulated by the entreaties of the victim to continue with all his strength for the conversion of sinners and the salvation of the world.

Who could have imagined that the blessed had given himself up to these fearful nightly punishments? In the course of the day, nothing seemed to alter the joy and the serenity of his smile. His gentle care of the sick, the ingenuity of his charity, his patience, his courage, Martin always showed his good humor to the persons he met.

Nor could anyone suspect, while meeting him in the streets of the city where he wandered with a radiant smile to works of charity, that he wore a metal chain tightly wound around his waist and that a hair shirt covered his bloodied shoulders.

The Fraternal Life of Brother Martin on Meeting Brother John Macias

Very humble, sociable in the genuine meaning of the word, helpful on demand, Blessed Martin was pleased to visit religious friends and joyfully discussed with them the Kingdom of God. These visits to Franciscans or the Dominicans of St. Mary Magdalen were the occasion of hearty thanks.

Brother John Macias was a lay-brother at the convent of St. Mary Magdalen, and in some way, a disciple of Brother Martin who was sixteen years older. The two entertained the same desire for holiness and witnessed the same generosity. Son of a noble Spaniard completely ruined, Brother John had first been a shepherd in his country, then, under divine inspiration, sailed for the new world. Unlike the Spanish soldiers eager for gold and riches, Blessed John left in his wake across South America the imprint of his good example. Finally, when arrived in Lima, he distributed to the needy the resources he had acquired from his labors, and went to the convent of St. Mary Magdalen to request humbly his admission as a lay brother. He was accepted immediately. The behavior of the new postulant was so edifying that right after his year of novitiate, he was entrusted with the task of porter (doorman). Like Blessed Martin, he distributed alms. The rich Peruvians and notables from Mexico gave him considerable sums destined for the needy; so much so that Brother John was able to satisfy the needs of countless indigents who, every day, filed past the door of the convent. He, too, did not know rest; his natural goodness did not fail. From every side, his counsels and opinions were requested. He ceaselessly encouraged his visitors to place greater confidence in Christ.

In the course of earthquakes, which from time to time shook the city of Lima, Brother John assembled the religious of the convent, dissuading them from fleeing to the garden. "Come with me to the chapel of the Rosary," he would say; "I assure you that no accident will ever occur." And, from then on, in similar circumstances, the religious got used to take refuge in that chapel dedicated o the Mother of God. They were always preserved from danger. The poor were pleased to attend his religious instructions. He knew how to evangelize by the excellent charm of his simplicity, strengthening them, and lifting them up by his purity. His lessons did not come from book learning. From experience, he spoke the language of faith and of love. It is easy to understand the nature of the conversations that united these two holy Brothers, both of them endowed with equal and ardent compassion for persons in need. With what fervor they must have praised their beloved Queen, Our Lady of the Holy Rosary!

At the end of their talk, Martin and John would retreat to a corner of the garden; there, absorbed in prayer, in silence, they implored the Lord to bless the apostolate of mercy and of compassion that was to dear to them.

[Note] Blessed Martin was also a close friend of St. Rose. According to Brother Francisco del Arco [Apostolic Process Book III, page 671 et seq.], she sometimes came to the door of the sacristy to consult with Brother Martin on spiritual matters. He called her Rosita, the little Rose.

Their lives were strikingly alike, even though one was of noble lineage, the other of modest origins and of the Black race. Both of them experienced the same success in their works of charity and of compassion. God was pleased to recognize their apostolic zeal, providing them with the funds needed for the relief of the poor and of the sick, by favoring them with the gift of miracles and of prophecy. Thus were they marked to be beatified one day by Pope Gregory XVI.

Compassion, Source of Thorough Humanity

It has been calculated that some one hundred sixty persons received nourishment from the hands of the holy religious. Every week, he distributed more than two thousand dollars to ward off their basic needs. How could he have this money at his command? You have to understand that the Spaniards who came to Peru were not all adventurers or bloodthirsty individuals. A good number of them, owners of immense fortunes acquired by barbaric methods and devoid of all scruples, would not lack generosity, even prodigality, regarding the victims of their conquest. The *conquistadores* did not save nor did they place money at interest; when facing death, they delighted poor people and religious with their bounty. Even though he was an inspired organizer, the Blessed did not limit his exercise of Christian charity to the unprofitable show of cold statistics.

Despite his extraordinary activity, Martin managed to reserve, at specific moments of the day and the night, seven hours of prayer, during which it happened many times that he be transported into ecstasy. Humble Brother Martin, moved to compassion for even the lowliest creatures, was favored with visits from the fortunate who recognized in him he promise of Christ: The humble will be exalted.

Prayer to St. Martin de Porres

5. Repentance

> Merciful God, who has given us the humble Brother Martin as an example of repentance and of mortification, watch over us and overlook our unfaithfulness!
>
> And you, very untainted Martin who not only suffered with resignation your sacrifices and your illnesses but also mortified harshly your innocent body: pray the Lord that he grant us a spirit of repentance so that we might receive with joy the mortifications as well as the humiliations from our fellows along with our own misfortunes so that, purified from our sins, God will protect us and receive us in his love and grant us always his powerful protection.
>
> Amen.

CHAPTER ONE

6. The Marvelous Displacements of Martin

The mission and the service of the blessed among the poor and the sick were so efficacious and agreeable to God that he allowed Martin to escape from the laws of nature, carrying him beyond the seas, to faraway places, and, in addition, to have him cross the limits of time.

A singular event, so to speak, in the annals of hagiography, and related to a fairy tale. And yet, three centuries after his death, his mission of mercy and compassion continue in America, according to the testimony of thousands of persons who benefit from it.

Let us take a visit back to the convent of the Holy Rosary of Lima, such as it was three hundred years ago. Brother Martin was infirmarian when an epidemic struck. Sixty novices were affected. The blessed "angel of mercy as much as of compassion" hastened to offer them all the care possible. You can imagine how often he was called, how often he had to be everywhere! When the door to the novitiate was closed, you could see Brother Martin enter and leave noiselessly. He went from one bed to the other, aware of each one's desires without their having to tell him. It was not even necessary to make him come: his intuition was enough for him to go where his presence was needed. Numerous testimonies were presented and introduced at his cause for beatification authenticating these various supernatural interventions.

One night, for example, a religious from the novitiate needed his help. The door was locked (as usual). Nonetheless Martin was no less at the bedside of the patient. Perhaps his guardian angel supported him with his vigilant help in these marvelous visits to the sick religious.

Another night, a novice, Francisco Verasco, felt himself so sick that he thought he would die. Alone, with no help, he was stricken with great distress. Suddenly, Brother Martin entered his room, carrying what he needed to comfort and treat young patient. The novice, in his surprise, asked him: "How could you know that I was sick?" – "No useless questions," answered Brother infirmarian; "be comforted, you will not die of it." Brother Francisco felt himself immediately healed. Many years later, having become a priest, he presented under oath the details of blessed Martin's visit. The Master of Novices, who had been apprised, could not contain his astonishment. "It is strange,"said he; "the door of the novitiate was certainly locked when you received this visit from Brother Martin. I locked the doors myself, as usual, and I held the keys."

Subsequently, the Master of Novices sought to explain the manner of these unusual visits. Pursuing his investigation, one night, around ten o'clock, after he had locked the two doors to the novitiate, he became aware of the presence of Brother Martin in the room of the sick novice. "But, how could he have entered? We'll see, at least, how he will leave." At that, the Master of Novices hid himself in an alcove to watch the movements of Brother Martin. Eyes fixed on the door of the room, he waited... A fruitless wait; no one appeared. He checked and found the doors securely locked, as usual. He touched the keys, still attached to his belt.... Surprised, he glorified God. According to records, Martin's attentiveness in favor of the sick novices was such that he had hoped to provide them with the fruit they dreamed of in their feverish state, even if the were out of season, or in fact, exotic.

One night, Rodrigo Melendez, struck with erysipelas (an infectious skin disease usually affecting the face, but not exclusively - Trans.) was suffering more than usual. "Ah! Who will bring some hot water to wash my leg," he moaned in a loud voice, moved more by pain than by confidence in the effectiveness of his appeal. It was heard by a diocesan priest, residing in the convent as a favor, wrapped in sleep, moreover in a distant room that he himself had locked from the interior. Rodrigo had barely uttered his complaint that Brother Martin was standing by his side, bringing him some hot water. To the questions besetting him from the sick person, he answered simply that he knew what to do to get to the bed of a sick person, whenever necessary. Father Juan Melendez reported the fact during the process of beatification.

Note: Son of Rodrigo Melendez, Father Juan Melendez, OP, was the author of a remarkable work concerning the Dominicans in the South during the first century of the Spanish conquest. Rodrigo was staying in the convent until such time as he could settle his debts and thus avoid arrest.

He was also witness to another miracle. Having come to get news about Father Juan de Salinas, ill in the infirmary — he had just suffered a hemorrhage of the stomach — the latter began to say to him: "What would I give to have a glass of sweetened water to appease my thirst." He had barely expressed this desire, when Brother Martin was at his side, bringing a glass of sweetened water, without the door ever opening!

Martin's Gift of Ubiquity

In his youth, Martin dreamed of going to evangelize the Yellow race in the Far East; his entrance into the Order had only strengthened that desire. But the missionary calling was not exactly his. Yet God, knowing the impartiality of Martin's zeal, allowed this wonderful missionary— to travel on many occasions to Mexico, Algeria, France, the Philippines, perhaps even to China — in the blink of an eye and unknown to everyone. Martin de Porres lived all his life in Lima, at the convent of the Holy Rosary. And yet, numerous and credible were the tokens that marked his presence over the entire world, among the poor, the captives, and the distressed, to help and comfort them.

A Creole, having returned from China where he had sojourned a long time, engaged in a very interesting conversation with Martin de Porres concerning Chinese customs, that the latter knew about as much as he did.

Francisco de Montoya knew the blessed in Africa, nursing and comforting numerous Christian slaves. Neither he nor his companions ever knew the identity of that mysterious missionary; but they affirmed with conviction that it was indeed Martin, who by his alms and his encouragement had relieved their distress and their captivity. We can easily appreciate the joy of Francisco, after his release from servitude and his return to Peru, when he suddenly met this benefactor in the church of the Holy Rosary. He fell into his arms, asked a thousand questions about his trip to Algiers. Martin replied evasively. But Francisco, intrigued, wanted to solve this mystery. Light was soon shed on the subject when the Prior vouched that the good Brother had never made a trip to Africa. One can imagine the enthusiasm of Francisco for this miraculous form of mission and of service, as well as his care to make this known throughout the world.

It is also possible that Martin de Porres came to France through this supernatural route. One day, while giving to a patient a medicine unknown in Peru, he spontaneously made this remark: "Take this, it is good. I saw this used in France, at a hospital in Bayonne."

A merchant in Lima never tired of repeating that before he left for Mexico, he had made it a point to recommend himself to the prayers of Brother Martin, in whom he had great confidence. After his arrival in the capital of Mexico, he fell grievously sick. His state was hopeless. In the throes of his agony, he cried out: "O God, why is Brother Martin not here to nurse me?" A that very instant, the good brother entered his room. A cheerful smile brightened his face. "How long have you been here?" asked the happy merchant. "I have just arrived," replied the visitor. Surveying the room, putting things in order with good humor and simplicity, he then said to the patient: "Oh man of little faith; why did you think you were about to die?" And, while giving him some medicine, he added: "Now, rest assured that you will not die of this fever." And Martin disappeared. The merchant soon recovered his health, and, wishing to thank his friend for his goodness, went in haste to the Dominican convent of Mexico, thinking that Brother Martin was staying there. No one had seen him. Where then could he be staying? The merchant searched fruitlessly in all the hotels of the city. No one had any knowledge of his having come. Accordingly, he had to await his return to Lima for news about Martin; but the religious at Holy Rosary assured him that Brother Martin had never left the convent.

The Brother "Invisible and Flying"

The blessed was equally given the gift of invisibility: whether he acted without being seen, or that in certain ecstasies he disappeared from the eyes of men. Even more extraordinary is the fact that he had the power to share this gift. Police agents had discovered in the convent the presence of two accused men. They were about to execute a warrant for the arrest of the accused when Brother Martin made the latter invisible, thereby allowing them to slip out of the hands of the police.

On another occasion, the invisible world that accompanied the blessed stealthily lifted the veil of his mystery. The religious of his community affirm having seen, one night, two angels standing by his side, at an hour, when according to custom, they used to return to the dormitory to recite the Little Office of the Blessed Virgin before Matins. Or else, throughout the cloisters, they saw Brother Martin, framed by four angels, looking like four handsome youths, carrying torches.

During a serious illness of Father Barragan, the bell-ringer awaited the fixed time to ring Matins when, all of a sudden, he saw Brother Martin flying in space, enveloped by a ball of fire. The latter was heading for the bedside of the patient. Or again, in the sight of the entire community, the blessed, in a flash had crossed from the chapter hall to choir.

Just as he shared with others his gift of invisibility, this "flying Brother," as he was called, was pleased one day to communicate his gift of speed to thirty novices whom we was leading on a walk. Martin had lost track of time, enchanted at seeing these young recruits take such pleasure in gamboling in the woods. Surprised by the evening, how was one to return to the convent at the appointed hour? A moment of perplexity for Brother Martin. What to do? The hour for office was about to ring; being far from the convent, the novices feared a reprimand. Martin began praying with all his heart and a ray of light bathed his face when he addressed the anxious group. "Come with me!" – Would they walk Indian file with Martin in the lead? Or else, holding on to each other by the hand and closing their eyes... then, one, two, three! - "Open your eyes!" A few steps and they would suddenly be at the threshold of the convent? We would very much like to have some enlightenment on this mystery. Who will ever know? The rather long distance was covered in less time than it takes to recount the feat. And that is not all: they cleared the already closed doors without bothering anyone. At the appointed time, they had taken their place in choir for the recitation of the Rosary!

Prayer to St. Martin de Porres

6. The Gifts from God

O glorious St. Martin, we thanks the Lord for the great power he deigned to grant you over life and death to help persons in need throughout the entire world.

Encouraged by the generosity with which you spread the gifts of God, we come to you with the greatest confidence. Obtain for us more faith, more love for God, along with the graces that we need.

We expect everything from your intercession on our behalf, to the glory of Our Lord Jesus Christ.

Amen.

7. Martin's Other Miracles

For nine years, Martin remained a tertiary in the Order of St. Dominic. In spite of his humility, out of obedience he was asked to submit to the will of his superiors that called for him to pronounce solemn vows, so that his consecration to God be more perfect. He understood that without himself preaching in the pulpit or assuming priestly functions, he could nonetheless effectively participate in the apostolate of the convent by assuring in love the different tasks indispensable for the proper advance of the community in the service of all his brothers: the care of the sick, the maintenance of rooms and hallways, the appearance of the clothes closet, along with those thousand and one needs encountered in community life in an important convent such as was that of the Holy Rosary. Martin understood that his mission and service among the poor and the sick was one way of collaborating in the ministry of the religious priests.

Fraternal Life in Community

More than three centuries later, our Constitutions confirmed the testimony of Brother Martin de Porres: The ministry of preaching is a community task, it is first of all the work of the entire community. Besides, originally the convent was called "Holy Preaching." The cooperator Brothers took part in the apostolate and in the mission of the whole community, not only by their work to serve the needs of the convent, but also by their ministry properly so-called, namely, whether they collaborated with the Brothers-priests, or whether they exercised an apostolic activity adapted to them." For the Friars Preachers, to live in community is like the source of their life. There, they draw at the same time the joy of fraternity like hope for the world, the benevolent support and critique for the mission, the environment for their human and spiritual conversion. Community life remains for us the road a two-fold adventure.

A human adventure, because fraternal life is the promise to which we wish to convert ourselves; it is also a concrete requirement that invites us to receive each other as brothers, beyond ideals.

An adventure of faith, because it is for a life given in fulness by Christ that we take on this challenge. Thus, through the gift of mercy and the shared search for truth, fraternity gradually becomes transformed.

"Just as in the Church of the Apostles, communion between us is based, built, and strengthened in the same Spirit: in Him, we receive the Word of God the Father in the same belief, we contemplate Him with the same heart, and praise Him with the same voice. In Him, we form a single body, and share the same bread; in Him, finally, we hold everything in common and we are destined for the same work of evangelization. [*Constitutions, the Common Life*]."

Do we have to show that the entire life of Brother Martin was a living and active preaching, convincing and attractive, edifying by the example of personal as much as supernatural virtues with which he was supplied by the providence and grace of the Lord?

Like St. Catherine of Siena, Blessed Martin enjoyed, among other gifts of the Holy Spirit, that of wisdom and a particular and certain sense of Catholic Theology, without the need, to be sure, of comparing him to St. Thomas Aquinas, the Angelic Doctor. One day, he overheard the lively discussion of two students concerning the essence and existence of God. The issue was to learn, according to our human manner of thinking, which was the highest perfection. Martin interjected this remark: "My children, go read what St. Thomas wrote on this point and you will find that, according to our human manner of thinking, existence is the highest perfection because it expresses in a single concept the complete Being of God." The students reported this reflection to Father Francisco of the Cross, Regent of Studies and Master in theology. The latter remarked: "Brother Martin is very learned; he possesses the knowledge of saints." On another occasion, in the course of a reasoning carried out between professors, Martin offered his word by indicating the reference in St. Thomas on the very question.

Even though the life of Blessed Martin abounded in miracles, one should not lose sight of his deep conviction concerning the need to fulfill the slightest tasks with rigorous promptness. The Rule and the Constitutions of the Order of St. Dominic traced the path for him to reach and live in community this call to sanctity, following Christ and our Father St. Dominic. It was because of his faithful observance, his patient charity, his sincere humility, his prompt obedience, that God granted him the gift of miracles.

Chapter One

Despite the assertions of some historians of the XVIIth century touching on strict observance of religious life among the Dominicans of South America, all the religious were far from being saints.

Brother Martin, on the other hand, as many reports reassure us, had the good sense of not forgetting his primordial duty, to work at his own sanctification and respond to the appeal of Christ: *convert yourself and believe the Good News*. This invitation is addressed to the entire Church and to each one of us. You, therefore, be perfect as your heavenly Father is perfect. [See *Mt* 5:48]. And besides, the will of God is our sanctification, St. Paul reminds us. [See *Eph* 1:4]. Occasionally, by discreet hints which he judged timely, the blessed did not fail to live the Gospel very simply every day of his religious life. One day, he saw a religious wearing a linen shirt and was annoyed by it. No doubt, to be dressed in attractive clothes was not blameworthy in itself, but the Dominican Rule forbade it. At first, he thought that the religious benefitted from a dispensation justified by some ailment; but when he learned that he wore linen because of a shortage of wool, he went from one haberdasher to another until he found enough material to make two or three shirts for each religious. Was this narrow-mindedness, a one-sided view?

Quite the contrary. He who wished to wear only old and patched clothing, surprised everyone by seeming to excuse the dress of a priest whose elegance had provoked the indignation of an older brother. "What do you think, Brother Martin, of such vanity, such frivolity on the part of a young priest?" – "It is a better sign than you think of the generous providence of God," replied Brother Martin. "God allows this nonchalance for a goal you do not know, and can use it for the conversion of sinners. Imagine a sinner, faint-hearted and unscrupulous — of which there are too many in the world — meeting this priest or someone like him; he will judge him to be easy-going toward hardened sinners, and if ever grace touches him, disposing him to repentance, he will hurry to go to the priest to confess and be reconciled to God. But suppose that one of those sinners dressed like you with a torn habit, wearing over-sized shoes with a countenance as grim as your own, eyebrows puckered, would he not run away, with no concern for the sins that weigh him down?"

Brother Martin had a liking for the novices, the hope of the Order and the blossoming of its missionary activity. One day, bending over one of them, sick and in bed, said to him: "Do you wish to live, little brother?" – "Yes," replied the young man. Martin added: "Good; you will not die of this illness. Live, my child, and work a long while for the conversion of sinners." The young novice was immediately restored to health.

Father Thomas de Rosario [of the Rosary], a religious of high virtue and on whom rested great hopes, died after a long illness. The Brothers were gathered to the recite the Office of the Dead, when Brother Martin entered into Brother Thomas's room. He closed the door and began to pray in a low voice at the feet of the crucifix, beseeching the Savior to manifest his mercy. Then, getting up, he approached the deceased and whispered into his ear: "Brother Thomas!" Immediately, he deceased moved slightly and emitted a sigh. A A witness to this miracle, Brother Ferdinand of Aragon, the doorkeeper, could not help but exclaim: "Oh, how powerful is God to return a dead person to life, at the request of a faithful servant." Martin slipped away and said to the Brothers assembled in the cloister: "You may now return to your rooms; Brother Thomas has come to his senses."

In 1634, a strong rise in the waters of the Rimac threatened to swallow up the church of Our Lady, built on its shores. Panic overtook the city. Moved, Martin ran to the river, chose three stones, in the name of the Trinity. He placed one on the shore of the swollen river, threw one a few paces at a distance, and the third into the middle of the torrent. After he had prayed fervently, under the eyes of an affected crowd, the river slowly returned to its normal level. The applause of the crowd echoed throughout the city. In gratitude, the citizens of Lima proposed to build a magnificent church at a place where floods would no longer be able to reach it. "Do no such thing," Brother Martin told them; "Notre Dame church was built where it was supposed to be. The Rimac would never again threaten it." A prophecy that was fulfilled.

Brother Martin's Gift of Prophecy

The gift of prophecy that Martin had regarded not only external events but also phenomena in the psychic order. He detected states of soul, revealed thoughts and emotions. Meeting for a first time Juan Ferrer, brother of a Dominican, he told him to his face "When will we see you with a biretta over your hair? This young man had formerly made a secret vow to join the Company of Jesus [Jesuits] if he were healed of a mental illness.

The foretelling of tragic events was also his business. An epidemic was raging in Lima; the infirmary of the convent was filled with sick religious. Fearing contagion or wishing to leave the Order, a novice pretended to be sick and requested permission to go home for treatment. Given the circumstances, the Prior could hardly refuse him. The young man was about to leave the convent, but Brother Martin had discovered the lie and the hidden intention. He stopped the novice, already on the stoop, pressing him to stay: "You pretend to be sick, You have abused the good faith of your superiors. Abandon that shameful and base plan." Martin's insistence aroused the ire of the novice, humiliated at having been detected, he turned aside with disdain from the one who was trying to save him. Seeing him obstinate in his foolish resolution, Martin told him: "Well, return home, dear Brother, God is waiting for you, but to punish you." The young man returned to his family, fell sick, and died.

The blessed had entrusted a student to take a letter to the convent of St. Francis. Being unscrupulous, the carrier allowed himself to open the letter, to learn its contents, then to reseal it carefully. But the matter did not escape the discernment of Martin, who reprimanded him for it. Father Cyprian de Medina reported that, in the absence of Brother Martin, in preparing a snack for him and his companions, some students had eaten the fruits they found in a drawer. One of them, unknown to he others, had even taken eight *reals* that he hid in his shoe. On his return, Martin told them: "My children, you have eaten the fruits that I had placed in the drawer; that was alright, I had saved them for you..." And turning to the guilty one he added: "As for you, you have to return to me the money that you took." Humiliated, the young man became indignant and impudent: "I do not have your money!" – Come now, my son, do not lie! Take the money out of your shoe and return it to me; it does not belong to you." The student complied.

Brother Martin was even more perceptive in identifying those who needed consolation. The Cyprian of Medina, mentioned above, suffered much during his novitiate because of his clumsiness and ugliness, and his companions hardly spared him. Martin's intuition was aware of the situation. Accordingly, one day he made this unusual prophecy to the novices: "You say that brother Cyprian is ugly because his face is not gracious and his members are deformed. He will become a very handsome man and will bring great honor to the Dominican Order." Six years later, the novice fell gravely ill. As he recovered, he could barely be recognized: he had grown a half-foot in height. Moreover, Brother Cyprian de Medina made constant spiritual progress, became Regent of Studies at the University of Lima, and subsequently, bishop of Huamanga. It was there that he died, well beloved by his people.

Martin had a special affection for this religious during the course of his illness. Brother Cyprian remarked to his nurse, who displayed paternal kindness toward him, "You consider me as your spiritual child, my dear Brother, and you leave me to myself, even though you know that I am at the threshold of death." – Rest assured," replied Brother Martin, with a smile, "when I make frequent visits to a patient, it is because he will not heal. Take courage. The Good Lord intends to prolong your life for his glory and service to our Order."

The Supernatural Gifts of Brother Martin

The supernatural gifts of the blessed served him well in the exercise of his charitable works. A Spaniard named Juan Gonzalez, condemned to be hanged, awaited the carrying out of his sentence. Martin went to the prison to comfort the unfortunate. The latter implored him to take care of his soul and to recommend him to God; this was done. On his return to the Priory, suddenly impelled by a new inspiration, Martin sent a message to the detained to tell him that he would not suffer the penalty of death. Now the decree had been final. The condemned had his foot on the scaffold, when fidgeting arose within the crowd. The wife of the Viceroy appeared on a balcony, hand raised, signaling to the executioner the pardon she was requesting in favor of the condemned. The request was acknowledged and the criminal, ghostly and shaking, was returned to prison. There he found forty dollars from Brother Martin, to pay for his immediate needs.

A stranger was dying in a hospital. How did Martin learn this? Only God knows. In the middle of the night, Brother appeared and told the nurse who was caring for the dying man: "He will die and has not received baptism." Turning to the stranger, he made known to him, as if by a lightning bolt, the state of his soul. The unfortunate man repented of having pretended to be baptized, confessed his sins, and became a Christian before dying.

Martin discovered the most secret thoughts, guilty intentions, undeclared feelings, as well as their causes. "Why that gloomy sadness," he asked Brother Ferdinand one day. "Be consoled; in fourteen years you will be freed from all your concerns." – "What concerns," said the brother, persuaded that his face could not reveal the cause of his anxiety. "Oh, I suppose that death will deliver me from them." – "No," replied Brother Martin; "it will not be death. You would like to become a priest; that you will be." At the time, Brother Ferdinand was a lay-brother, with no hope of ever being raised to priestly dignity, even though this apparently unrealizable desire haunted him. "When you return to Lima," Brother Martin continued, "you will no longer find me here." In fact, fourteen years later, Ferdinand was ordained priest in Santiago, Chile, and returned to Lima only after the death of the blessed.

Don Juan de Figuerra, Governor of Lima — to whom Martin had already made known several predictions — was waiting for many important documents from the Court of Spain. Martin quieted him, saying that they would arrive in a few days. Under other circumstances, he was able to convince the Governor that in spite of the intrigues being hatched against him by the Viceroy of Peru, he would occupy the post he had requested from the Finance Bureau of Potosì, which did come to pass even though Don Juan had lost all hope. Moreover, Martin revealed to him that he would experience many calamities but that he would bear them courageously and that they would be a rich source of merit for him. In fact, it was not long before the unfortunate Governor was overwhelmed with diverse ordeals. He lost a hundred thousand dollars in revenue. Because of serious concerns concerning health, he became weak. When he was at the end of his strength, mean-spirited slanderers set to work at ruining his reputation. Given the realization of the prophecies that had been made, he called for Martin. "Promise me that you will pray for me when I am about to die..." – "I will die before you," was the answer he heard. While he was having prepared in the church of Mercy a chapel richly decorated to harbor his last sleep, the Governor submitted his plans to Brother Martin. "Prepare that chapel," he latter replied, "but do no be concerned about your right to be buried there. That will not be the place of your repose, but right here, in our convent, next to me." This answer must have astounded Don Juan de Figuerra. But fourteen years after the death of Brother Martin, the Dominicans transformed the room of the blessed into a chapel, along with the nearby rooms and asked the Governor to place the sanctuary under his patronage. The old man understood then the meaning of the prophecy that was fulfilled to the letter. At his death, Don Juan was buried beside his saintly friend.

Brother Martin's Gift of Compassion

Compassion is an abstract notion. Immediately, every one of us creates a mental image different from that of his neighbor. To give flesh to this subjective feeling, and to give it meaning, we look for visible manifestations of compassion.

Within his Dominican community at Lima, Brother Martin remained the model of all compassion. He was either always cited as an example or his kindness — as patient as it was foreseeing — called upon to resolve delicate problems and receive persons in the depths of misfortune or wounded by life. In his religious life, he put into practice what the apostle Paul reminded the Christians of Colossa to encourage them especially in fraternal life. Wrap yourselves in feelings of tender compassion, in kindness, humility, patience... In all humility, kindness, and patience, bear with one another in charity. [See *Col* 3:12].

Dictionaries agree in saying that compassion is the feeling we experience when another is facing distress or a misfortune. At that time, we go to pity the individual and to find some way of sharing his suffering. Historically, the Latin word *compassio* is derived from *compati*, literally, to suffer with.

Prayer to St. Martin de Porres

7. The Christian Calling

> O my God, who are so generous with him who loves you in all sincerity and with all his heart heart, we love you and we wish to love you even more. Through the intercession of St. Martin, may our love for you grow ever stronger.
>
> And you, blessed Martin, pray for us and obtain that we may reach the love of God that will allow us to live out our Christian calling.
>
> Obtain for us also the graces we need and which we expect from your powerful intercession to Our Savior. Amen.

Chapter Two

St. Martin de Porres
- His death on 3 November 1639 at the convent of the Holy Rosary of Lima
- His beatification on 29 November 1837 by Pope Gregory XVI in Rome
- His canonization on Sunday 6 May 1962 by Pope John XXIII in Rome
- Readings proposed for the feast of St. Martin de Porres on 3 November

No one among us lives for himself and no one dies for himself. If we live, we live for the Lord; if we die, we die for the Lord. In life and in death, we belong to the Lord. If Christ has known death then life, it was to become the Lord of the dead and of the living. [See Rom 14:7-8.]

1. The Holy Death of Brother Martin

In 1639, Don Feliciano de Vega, Archbishop of Mexico, traveling in Lima, suddenly had to take to bed. He suffered from acute pleurisy. His state seemed hopeless. He found at his bedside Father Cyprian of Medina, his nephew, who asked him why he had not thought of having Brother Martin come to him. The worthy prelate, well disposed to abandon himself to the ministrations of the humble brother, entreated his nephew to ask the Prior of the convent of the Holy Rosary to send him along. Pleased to be able to be of service to the Archbishop of Mexico, the Prior sent someone to look for Brother Martin. Nobody knew where he was. Several calls from a bell were unanswered. The unrest spread throughout the community. Don Feliciano was about to die... Where could Brother Martin be? For three hours, some groups throughout the city set out to look for him. All in vain. Then Father Cyprian had a sudden inspiration: he suggested to the Provincial that, in the name of holy obedience, the brother come to join them in the sacristy. The Provincial agreed, and immediately Brother Martin was seen to appear mysteriously. The Provincial ordered him to go to the Archbishop and to obey him as he did his religious superiors.

In agony, the Prelate reproached Martin for his delay in coming, and asked him to place his hand on his very painful side. To have been considered as a miracle-worker offended his humility. "How could Your Excellency condescend to ask that of a poor insignificant brother? – "My dear Brother," replied the Archbishop, "your Provincial has commanded you to obey me; place your hand on my side, I order you in the name of holy obedience." Martin complied and the relief was instantaneous. The healing was so prompt and so complete that Don Feliciano made arrangements to return immediately to Mexico and attempted to obtain from the Provincial permission to take brother with him. The company of such a miracle-worker would be security for him during the trip back. The Provincial consented, but with regrets; both of them expected Brother Martin to leave without delay. These arrangements must have brought a smile to the religious who was aware of his future.

The Final Contest of Brother Martin

In fact, just a few days later, the Procurator met Brother Martin, wearing a new habit but of coarse cloth. "Why are you wearing a new habit," he asked him. "It will be the habit in which I will be buried," replied Martin in a calm voice. Soon after, a fever struck him and obliged him to get to bed. "Here comes the end of my earthly pilgrimage. I will die from this sickness; no medicine will be able to cure me." No one believed him. Efforts were made to reduce his temperature. And preparations of a simple remedy were made. Martin rejected them, saying: They will not soothe me in any way; the hour of my death has arrived."

The blessed received the last sacraments with much fervor and humility, afer having experienced physical sufferings. According to his prediction, the fever doubled in intensity, and brought him unspeakable torments. Then, the devils set upon him, feeble and in anguish as he was, in attempt to scare him, to get him to give in to pride and to fall into unbelief. A Father, doctor in theology, enlisted the dying man not to discuss anything with the enemy, simply to hold on to faith and to renew his confidence in the Lord. Martin traced a smile: "Satan is too prideful to engage in fine points with a simple lay brother like me."

Every beat of his faithful heart pushed away the infernal temptations. His body was bathed in sweat; his teeth chattered. The legions of Satan set upon him with ferocious energy to reawaken in him the unconquered leavings of human weakness. But the unfortunate, in a dying voice, confided the great consolation he had in being helped in his agony by the Mother of God, St. Joseph, St. Dominic, St. Vincent Ferrer, and St. Catherine of Alexandria. When the hour came to wish him a final "God be with you," Martin reacting to the sound of the bell calling the community, following Dominican custom, advised the Superior with a gesture not to disturb anyone. Taking no notice of his wishes, the religious gathered around his bedside. Brother Martin made a final effort to ask pardon for what he called his "poor example." The prayers for the dying were recited. The blessed, face bathed in tears, covered with kisses the crucifix he held in his hands. At his request, the community recited aloud the Creed. At the moment the words *who was conceived of the Holy Spirit and born of the Virgin Mary*, he closed his eyes and fell asleep quietly in the peace of the Lord. Blessed Martin died at 9 in the evening on 3 November 1639, at the age of sixty, in the thirty-sixth year of his religious profession.

The news of his death spread like a trail of gunpowder, causing a night of sorrow throughout the country. The Peruvians could tell themselves that they would now have a powerful protector in heaven, but there would now be something changed in Lima. No longer would Brother Martin be met in the streets, burdened with bread, fruit, and medicine. No longer would his words of comfort be heard. Whom had he not helped, protected, strengthened: Spaniards, Blacks, Indians, old men and children, young girls and mothers of families, poor and rich, priests and civil servants? All of them owed him heartfelt gratitude. From one end of the city to the other, even beyond, far beyond, where his charity had spread, deep sadness overcame hearts.

He would no longer smile at children, no longer provide food and clothing to persons in need, no longer console the hopeless, no longer visit prisons and hospitals, nor orphanages that he had helped to build. All that was left to do was to visit Holy Rosary convent to view for a last time the remains of him who had always been held in reverence as a saint. A dense crowd filed before the casket of Brother Martin, laid out in a temporary chapel. The sorrow caused by the loss of a benefactor was evident — no longer to see him fulfilling his mission of mercy, but to see him lying there, frozen in death... Was this in fact real?

The Miracles of Brother Martin

It was then that occurred an event as uncommon as it was marvelous. One evening, Father Cyprian de Medina, moved to see the body of his friend bound by the rigidity of death, and concerned about proclaiming the glory of God and the holiness of blessed Martin, had the sudden inspiration of addressing him a friendly reproach. "How is it, Brother Martin, that your body be rigid? The entire population of Lima, in the presence of your casket, awaits miracles to glorify the Lord. Ask God, therefore, to manifest his power by making your body more supple." The spirit of faith in Father Cyprian found its reward in an immediate miracle. The body of the blessed became supple is if he were alive. The aroma of lilies and of roses suddenly filled the chapel.

The crowd could not contain its enthusiasm and rushed near the revered remains. From everywhere, from Lima to its surroundings, people flocked in, invaded the convent for several days. Many times, it was necessary to replace the habit of the deceased: the faithful were not content with simple placing on it of their rosaries or their medals. They reduced the rough serge habit to shreds. The priests, in consideration first of all of the honor given to the Servant of God closed his eyes.... The unending affluence delayed the date of the funeral. The obsequies unfurled in great ceremony.The Archbishop of Cuzco, the Count of Chinchon, the Viceroy of Peru, and Juan de Pennafield, member of the royal household, carried on their shoulders the bier of the humble Dominican lay-brother, escorted by a procession of knights, prelates, priests from all the religious Orders, followed by an immense crowd of women, men, and children. Burial was held in the chapter hall. Miraculous healings occurred one after another. Already, in the temporary chapel, at the simple contact with the casket, Lady Catherine de Gonzalez, crippled for fifteen years, regained the use of her members. Lady Elizabeth of Astorga, on contact with the tunic worn by the blessed, was delivered from fevers reportedly incurable. Elizabeth Orhez de Torrez, on kissing an image of Brother Martin, addressed this prayer to him: "Venerable Brother, you supported me when you were on earth; now that you are in heaven, do not abandon me!" She was immediately relieved of neuralgias from which she suffered terribly. A Black, Juan Criollo, having imbibed some water containing dust from the casket suddenly experienced complete deliverance from the intolerable fevers that assailed him.

The intervention of Martin de Porres, invoked in hopeless cases, was made known by instantaneous improvements. Here is an example. Doctor Diego de Cevallos, afflicted with laryngitis and dysentery, was on the point of dying. He received the last sacraments. A relic of the blessed was brought to him, which in confidence he applied on his throat. He began to pray then fell into a deep sleep. Eight hours later, he woke up in perfect health. The astonished physicians could attribute this sudden cure only to a miraculous intervention. From that time on, a large number of the faithful accustomed themselves to go to Holy Rosary convent, to ask for the help of blessed Martin. The blessings and the favors obtained by his intercession became so numerous that the judges and the clergy suggested to the religious that they transfer the remains of the blessed to a more accessible chapel. The very room of the servant of God, beside the stoop of the convent, seemed appropriate to this goal and therefore the construction of a chapel was undertaken.

The transfer was made secretly on a night of March 1664, a year during which was to be celebrated the twenty-fifth anniversary of Martin's death. The disinterment took place in the presence of Count of St. Stephen, then viceroy of Peru, members of the royal household, and other civil authorities, members of the chapter of the Cathedral, several members of the diocesan and regular clergy. The body was intact and gave off a very agreeable perfume. The flesh, by its appearance and constitution, was similar to that of a living body. Upon examination, skillful men saw appear from their punctures drops of red blood. In the intimacy of that sensitive circle, the holy body was placed in a sarcophagus, in the shadow of a small dome, erected in the chapel.

The Beatification of Martin de Porres

From that time on, the entire world took an interest in the heroic life of the humble mulatto who was eager to help men by means of his miraculous gifts. In gratitude for the benefits obtained through his intercession, a considerable number of people prayed for his beatification. Moreover, Phillip IV, who had already sent two letters to Pope Alexander VII and to his Ambassador in Rome, on 17 December 1650 and 20 June 1661, sent a third letter, expressing the same request. The Archbishop of Lima also wrote to the Holy See, asking for the beatification of Martin de Porres. The chapter of the Cathedral, the civil and religious authorities of the city, the Order of St. Dominic, joined their requests to his own. Pope Clement IX considered these petitions when authorizing the pursuit of the process.

Unfortunately, the ship carrying the pontifical letters sank in the Mediterranean, near the port of Naples. Some days after the shipwreck, a case of papers was retrieved from the ship. Only the pontifical documents were intact. Other mishaps delayed further the movement of the process. Francis Blanco, the notary charged with putting into writing the depositions concerning the life and the miracles of Martin, was suffering so much from ulcers on his feet that he was unable to get the deposition of the most important witness: the Archbishop of Santa Fe, Don Juan de Ariguinao, who was preparing to return to his diocese. The ill-fated notary turned to the blessed, praying him to consider his impotence and fell asleep. The following morning, on awaking, he saw his wounds healed up and was thereby able to go to the prelate.

And here we meet again Juan Vasquez, who for four years, as we remember, was helper and companion to Martin in his works of mercy. Juan had left for Spain before the death of the blessed, who in making his farewells predicted to him that he would not see him again on this earth, at least in a normal fashion. "Farewell, my dear child, we will not see each other again in this world, or else you will not believe your eyes." As confidant of the blessed, Juan was able to offer in favor of the cause a testimony of great value, in which he did not hide anything but whose brevity baffled somewhat the judge who had asked for it. Besides, he incurred a strange and mysterious reproach for having been so laconic in his declarations that after his deposition and while he was praying in his room, he heard his name called from outside Looking out the window, he saw two religious pass by, silent and meditative. "I must be mistaken," he thought; "no one has called me." Kneeling down, he continued his prayers. Suddenly, he was startled; someone had called him. It was the same voice in the street. He saw he same two religious, approached them, and asked if they had called him. "Juan Vasquez," said one of them; "do you not recognize me?" Stunned, he recognized Brother Martin, dead for so long! "Why were you so reserved in your depositions concerning my life?" added the blessed. "Go, tell them all you have seen and heard; reveal everything you know!" Juan saw in this criticism the realization of a prediction that Martin had made to him before his boarding ship for Spain. Even though he was comforted by this incredible vision, he delayed, either by negligence or by natural timidity, to execute the order received. The unpublished details that he could have furnished would have slowed down the movement of the process; but he did nothing about it. Father Bernard de Medina had to go find him to obtain the documentation he needed to compose a biography of Martin de Porres. Vaquez was undoubtedly as laconic as usual because Father Bernard made him promise that he would remember everything he had witnessed and submit it to him.

This was in 1671, forty years after Juan had left for Spain. The cause was introduced solemnly in 1668, at the Congregation of Rites, under Pope Clement IX. It was considered a sure thing, but important testimony from the boy who helped Martin with his works of charity was lacking. Finally, on a morning of February, Juan Vasquez decided to give to the biographer the story of Martin's ecstasies, his visions, the splendid nights, his miracles and the incomparable charity that he had witnessed for four years. He walked silently, absorbed in his thoughts, careful to learn whether, truly, he was expected to tell everything he knew; would he not be drawing attention on himself? Suddenly, he found himself nose to nose with Martin de Porres, on the road, in full daylight. "Why," Martin reproached him, "have you paid so little attention to my orders? Go right now, and relate all you know." Martin had been dead thirteen years at the time of this second apparition. It served to emphasize to Juan the importance of his deposition and convinced him to leave out nothing that he could remember. Father Bernard de Medina recorded the facts very meticulously. All that we know about Martin de Porres comes from this first biography and from testimonials given under oath during the ecclesiastical process from 1658 to 1686.

Nonetheless, it was only on 29 April 1763 that the apostolic decree, issued by Pope Clement XIII, proclaimed the heroic nature of Martin de Porres's virtue. The important news was announced publicly in the course of a solemn office celebrated in the cathedral, in the presence of the Viceroy, the Archbishop, civic, military, and ecclesiastical authorities, along with an immense crowd. All of them shed tears joy because it was almost the hour that their beloved Brother Martin would be beatified. The virtues and the miracles of the holy man of God were brought to mind. More than one hundred sixty witnesses of the miraculous events were interviewed in the course of the inquiry for the process. The files were sealed before the assembly of the faithful. Unable to hold back his emotions, the Archbishop declared: "This is how God honors this man of color who knew how to love and serve him with all his heart."

Chapter Two

Finally, on 31 July 1836, Pope Gregory XVI published the decree of approbation, and on 8 August 1837, signed the apostolic letters of beatification. On 29 October 1837, Martin de Porres, the humble lay-brother, friend of the poor and the afflicted was solemnly declared *blessed servant of God,* to the joy of the entire Catholic world, full of enthusiasm and gratitude.

The ecclesiastical process leading to the canonization of Blessed Martin was taken up in Rome in 1926. Interest in his apostolate increased again in January 1935. The year 1937-1938 was marked by the first centenary of his solemn beatification. The enthusiasm in his favor, the devotion paid to him, the numerous benefits obtained through his intercession in the United States, Canada, England, Ireland, the West Indies, Mexico, the Philippines, in Africa and even in India, lead us to believe that Brother Martin had not abandoned his exceptional and heroic goodness toward the persons in need who called on him, and whom he always had at heart to help. Catholics and Protestants, Jews and pagan beseeched his help.

In an apostolic letter dated 10 June 1945, Pope Pius

XII declared Martin to be patron of social works in the Republic of Peru.

At St. Peter of Rome, on Sunday 6 May 1962, His Holiness [now St.] John XXIII, surround be a flock of important men and women of all races, all nationalities, come from all continents to glorify St. Martin de Porres, inscribed him in the Catalogue of Saints.

Prayer to St. Martin de Porres

8. At the Hour of Our Death

O Blessed St. Martin, you have seen how your various services, your mission, your mortifications, your charity and love for God were crowned by a holy death. Have pity on us and everyone who deplores the loss of you. Persons in need, the poor as much as the sick, believe they have lost a very compassionate brother and a remedy for their ills.

They cannot control their sorrow; your death has torn their hearts. Nonetheless, they are aware that you have not abandoned them. They call on you and you continue to help and comfort them in their distress.

You are near to the Lord, glorious St. Martin, and your influence remains ever stronger. Listen, then, to our humble prayers. Ask the Lord to protect us.

May our death be that of the just, thanks to your intercession and to the merits of Our Lord Jesus Christ.

Amen.

CHAPTER TWO

2. The Canonization of Brother Martin de Porres

On Sunday, 6 May 1962, in Rome, the basilica was filled with faithful from all countries. As on Pentecost, all languages could be heard. Spanish hymns arose, others came in relays. After a moment of silence, applause started up. The Pope entered, being carried on the ceremonial seat, and the crowd continued to applaud the successor of St. Peter. He moved slowly behind the banner on which was represented he who shortly would be inscribed in the catalogue of saints.

The Holy Father went to the throne set up at the end of the apse, took the chair of St. Peter, where he proclaimed solemnly the holiness of Brother Martin de Porres.

Then, the Holy Father recapitulated in major lines of his homily, the portrait of this saint of heaven who was offered to us as an example.

Homily of His Holiness [now Saint] John XXIII

For us, as for all Christians, the principal object of our concerns is the very important event that will be the Second Ecumenical Council of the Vatican. It brings about, in fact, the firm hope of a vigorous rejuvenation for the mystical Body of Christ, that is to say, the Church. It is toward him, before all, that everything is oriented, everything we are now doing and undertaking, we to whom the Very Holy Redeemer has entrusted on this earth his spotless spouse. Even today's solemn ceremony, in this majestic Vatican basilica, seems to fit perfectly, while we add to the number of saints a man of remarkable virtue. We wish to highlight that the most desirable action we could expect from the Council be that it move the children of the Church to decisions of greater holiness.

In fact, as Martin shows us by the examples of his life that we can achieve salvation and holiness by the path that Jesus Christ traced for us, namely: First, to love God with all our heart, with all our soul, with all our spirit, then to love our neighbor as ourselves. [See *Mt* 22:16-38.]

In this way, Martin, from his very childhood, loved God above all things, the gentlest of fathers, and gave proofs simple and sincere for which God Himself could only rejoice. After his admission into the Order of Dominicans, his piety was so strong that more than once, in the course of his prayers, he seemed carried to heaven, his soul having cut itself off from everything. Indeed, he had deeply engraved into his heart what St. Catherine of Siena expressed in this way: "It is natural that he who loves be loved in return. It has to be said that he who returns to his Creator love for love quenches His thirst" (Letter 8). Filled with this conviction that Christ Jesus suffered for us and that He carried our sins in his body on the cross [See *1 Pt* 2:21-24], he especially loved Christ crucified. When he meditated on the cruel sufferings, he could not help but shed abundant tears. He also had a special love for the Most Holy Sacrament of the Eucharist; often, in secret, he spent long hours adoring him in the tabernacle, and desired to feed himself with him as often as possible. His love for the Holy Virgin Mary was indescribable; he cherished her as his most gentle mother.

Moreover, in perfect obedience to his divine Master, Martin showed for his brothers a very generous charity, drawn from an undiluted faith and from the humility of his heart. He loved men because he sincerely saw in them the Son of God and his brothers. In addition, he loved them more than himself, because in his humility he judged them to be more just and better than he was. In sum, with these feelings he exhibited toward neighbors that benevolence befitting genuine heroes of the faith.

In fact, Martin excused the faults of others and forgave the most cruel of injuries because he was convinced that his sins deserved even greater punishment. He tried as hard as he could to bring sinners back to the right path. With kindness, he ministered to thesick. To the poor, he provided nourishment, clothing, and medicine. To peasants and Blacks, as well as to the mestizos — who, at the time, were considered as lowly slaves — he offered all his ministrations, and, to the degree possible, helped them, enveloped them with his attention, to the point that he deserved to be called *Martin of charity*. It must be noted that, in this, he followed his own system and ways of doing things, which at the time were absolutely new and prefigured those of our time. This is why our predecessor of happy memory, Pius XII, proclaimed Martin the patron of all social institutions that existed in the Republic of Peru. (Apostolic Letter, 10 June 1945.)

Martin walked with such enthusiasm in the footsteps of Christ that soon he achieved perfect and eminent virtue, to the point of offering himself as a sacrifice. At the call of the divine Redeemer, he embraced religious life to obligate himself by the bonds of a more perfect holiness. In his convent, he was not content to observe all that the vows he had pronounced called for, but he practiced chastity, poverty, and obedience so totally that his colleagues and his superiors saw in him the very embodiment of virtue.

The radiance of his holiness spread this charm and this goodness which, during life and even after his death, won him the hearts of everyone, whatever their race or nationality. It is because of this that we understand full well why this humble and impoverished child of Peru has been compared to St. Catherine of Siena — she who is regarded as the brightest star in the Dominican family, canonized five years ago. She was outstanding for her learning and the influence of her soul, he for conforming all his life to the way of living and of acting according to the precepts of Christ.

Venerable brothers and dear children, as we said at the beginning of this homily, we find it very timely that in the course of this year, which, as we have decreed, will see the celebration of the Ecumenical Council, the honors of saints be bestowed on Martin de Porres. Indeed, the heights of Christian holiness which he achieved, the magnificent and shining virtues of which his life gives a brilliant example, are such that we are able to see in them the healthful benefits that above everything else we hope for from this upcoming and among most solemn events, as much for the Catholic Church as for the whole human society.

This holy man, in fact, who by his words, his example and his virtues attracted so many men to religion, is able even now, three centuries after his death, admirably to draw our souls towards heaven. Alas, not everyone understands how necessary these goods of heaven are and do not value them. Much more, numerous are those who, attracted by the seductions of vice, despise them and turn away from them when they do not neglect them totally. May the example of Martin teach a great number of people, for the sake of their salvation, how pleasant and serene it is to follow in the footsteps of Jesus and to obey his divine commandments.

Here, venerable brothers and dear children, presented to your souls and traced in broad lines is the countenance of this saint chosen by heaven. Fix your attention on those admirable features, and each one of you, following your individual conditions, inspire your life with these eminent virtues, especially you young ones, full of enthusiasm, who in our days are threatened with so many dangers and trials. Before all, may the nation of Peru, so dear to us, find an example to be followed in those ancestral glories of the Catholic religion, and through the intercession of St. Martin de Porres, give the Church new examples of virtue and holiness. Amen. [Trans.]

The Canonization Mass

His Holiness, Pope (St.) John XXIII began the Mass, whose chants were sung by the choral group of the Sistine Chapel. At the elevation, he lifted up the host and the chalice for all to see as he turned himself to the right and to the left, while silver trumpets blared. The sacrifice of Christ was renewed for all the Christians of the entire world in the mystery of faith. The Church of the earth and that of heaven found themselves in exceptional union.

At 11:30, the immense crowd of pilgrims left the basilica and gathered in St. Peter's Square where at twelve o'clock from the window of the library, the Holy Father, who had just returned to his apartment, recited the *Regina Cæli* then addressed a few words especially to the pilgrims from Peru who had come in great numbers to honor St. Martin de Porres.

Chapter Two

Before leaving, the Pope granted his blessing to all the faithful and to the three-hundred ten cooperator brothers from the entire Order of Friars Preachers who had come to Rome especially for this event.

Audience for the Pilgrims Who Had Come for the Canonization of St. Martin de Porres

On Monday morning, 7 May 1962, by 7:30, the group of thiry-one cooperator brothers from the three provinces, of Toulouse, Paris, and Lyons, assembled beneath the banner *France* that identified us, near the bronze door through which we would enter the hall of audience. Contrary to custom, we crossed all the doors without waiting. Usually, pilgrims enter progressively and slowly through majestic galleries and great halls to reach the Hall of Blessings. His Holiness (St.) John XXIII had reserved this audience for the many pilgrimages which came from all continents for the canonization of Martin de Porres. Ten thousand pilgrims were assembled for this occasion. The central aisle of the great Hall of Blessings found itself quickly bordered by a row of cooperator Brothers: Peruvians, Frenchmen, Spaniards, Belgians, Canadians. At 9 AM, the Sovereign Pontiff entered, carried on the ceremonial chair [*sedia*] and cheered by the faithful.

In response to the address of homage by His Eminence Cardinal Juan Ladazuri Ricketts, Archbishop of Lima, His Holiness (St.) John XXIII immediately gave a speech in Spanish.

After having greeted the Cardinal Archbishop of Lima, the bishops present, the Peruvian and Spanish authorities, the Order of St. Dominic, and the numerous pilgrims who came from Peru and all the other countries, the Holy Father sang the praises of St. Martin de Porres.

Allocution of His Holiness (St.) John XXIII

Dear pilgrims.

Yesterday, a spring flower blossomed in the Church. A humble Dominican Brother who received the baptismal waters of baptism at the same font as St. Rose of Lima, has become the object of the highest honors of the Church. Let all the earth praise the Lord, admirable in His saints, who allowed us to be given this joy in which we also recognize a manifestation of our love for Peru, a nation rich in promise and in virtue.

Our most cordial congratulations to our dear Cardinal Archbishop of Lima, here present, to other members of the episcopate, to the high Peruvian and Spanish authorities, to the Dominican Friars, and to the numerous pilgrims from Peru and elsewhere.

In praising our saint, we wish to gather some traits that still preserve their full aroma of holiness after four centuries.

In the life of Brother Martin, there were three loves: Jesus crucified, Our Lady of the Rosary, and St. Dominic. Three passions burned in his heart: charity, especially toward the poor and the sick, very rigorous mortification that he considered "the price of love," and humility which fed his virtues. Allow me to dwell particularly on this last one and that we reflect on it in the transparent soul of Brother Martin.

Humility restricts the vision that man has of himself to its genuine limits as indicated by reason. It leads to its perfection the gift of fear of the Lord by which the Christian, aware that the Sovereign Good and its authentic grandeur are to be found only in God, pays him supreme respect and avoids sin, the only evil that can separate him from God. This is the key to the practical wisdom that regulates the life of prudent and discrete men. The fear of God is the school of wisdom the Holy Book tells us. [See *Prv* 15:33].

Chapter Two

Martin de Porres was the angel of Lima. In their difficulties, the novices confided in him; the most sedate Fathers sought his advice. He reconciled households, cured the most unyielding illnesses, appeased hatreds, resolved theological disputes, and gave his definitive opinion on most difficult matters. What wisdom, steadiness, and goodness in his heart! He was not a learned man but he possessed the true knowledge that ennobles the spirit, the *light of hearts* that God gives to those who fear Him, that *light of discretion* of which St. Catherine of Siena spoke (Letter 213). In his soul, there reigned the holy fear of God which is the foundation of all learning, of genuine spiritual progress, and in the long run, of civilization itself. The principle of wisdom is the fear of God. [See *Ps* 111:10.]

On seeing him raised to the glory of the altars, we admire Martin de Porres with the rapture of a man who gazes on a manificent panorama from the top of a mountain.

But it should not be forgotten that humility is the road that leads to such heights. *Humility precedes glory* [See *Prv* 15:33]. The higher the building, the deeper must be the foundations. Before rising up, the construction is brought low; before building the roof, a foundation has to be dug. [See Aug: *Serm. 10, De Verbum Domini.*] This is also the lesson that St. Martin gives us.

We address to him our hymn of praise and our prayers. Let us sing the praises of illustrious men and the fathers of our race... The people celebrate their wisdom and the assembly spreads their praises. [*Sir* 44:1, 15]. Let them bless Peru, the country that saw his birth; Spain that brought the Christian faith to the Americas, and the illustrious Order of Preachers. May the light of his life guide men on the road to Christian social justice and to universal charity with no distinction of color or of race. All of this is what we request, while with all our heart we offer to you yourselves, to your families and your loved ones our apostolic blessing. [Trans.]

Prayer to St. Martin de Porres

9. The Glory of God

O blessed Martin! On earth you lived only for God and your neighbors. Now, seated near the throne of goodness and mercy, you can more easily hand out your treasures. If here below you knew were to find our misfortune to bring it remedy, now you must see it better from the height of heaven where you reside.

Benevolent Martin, look down on those who come to you in the certitude that they will be heard. Do not disappoint the hopes of those who rejoice in seeing you glorified on earth and in heaven.

Amen!

CHAPTER TWO

3. Texts Proposed for the Office of Lessons on 3 November, Feast Day of St. Martin de Porres

The Kind Man Vouches for His Neighbor

Be indulgent toward the unfortunate, do no have them wait for alms. To obey the precept, come to the aid of the poor; he is in need: do not send him away empty-handed. Sacrifice your money for a brother and a friend so that it not rust in loss under a stone. Use your riches according to the precepts of the Most High; that will be more beneficial to you than gold. Store your alms in your barns; they will deliver you from all evil. Better than a strong shield, better than a heavy spear before the enemy, they will fight for you. [See *Sir* 20:11-27; 1:10.]

The kind man stands good for his neighbor; to abandon him is a sign of the absence of all shame. Do not forget the services of your patron. He gave his life for you. The sinner has no concern for the benefits from his patron; the ingrate forgets who it was that saved him. A pledge has ruined many happy persons and tossed them about like the waves of the sea. It exiled some powerful men who wandered among foreign nations. The wicked man who hastens to post bond in search of profit rushes forth to condemnation. Help your neighbor according to your ability and be careful not to fall yourself.

My son, do no refuse a poor man his subsistence and do not allow the unfortunate to languish. Do not make the hungry man suffer, do not inflame the indigent. Do not be obstinate against an angry heart, do not let the needy be bereft of your alms. Do not push away the unfortunate who is seriously tried; do not turn your gaze away from the poor person. Do not close your eyes to the needy, nor give anyone the opportunity to curse you. If someone, in his distress, curses you, the Creator will honor his oath. Make yourself loved by the community; before an exalted person, bow your head. Lend an ear to the poor man an grant him his welfare with kindness. Deliver the oppressed from the hand of the oppressor and do not be faint-hearted in rendering justice. Favor the orphans like a father and be like a husband to their mothers. Thus you will be a son of the Most High who will love you even more than your mother. [See *Sir* 29:15.]

The Variety of Gifts in the Church (from St. Catherine of Siena's Dialogue*)*

The soul inflamed by love for my truth which it seeks to have loved by everyone, collectively and individually, to varying degrees, ceaselessly contributes to the well-being of the entire world.

The union of love that it has contracted with me and that makes it love the universe inclines it to spread its love to the needs of the entire world. After having changed itself, by understanding the virtues that produce the life of grace, it strives to lift its eyes to the particular needs of its neighbors. When it begins to act in virtue of its love for charity towards all creatures with reason, it comes to help its neighbors according to the diversity of the gifts which I had given it to distribute. In fact, to one I give the virtue of teaching, to carry the word, by giving neighbors appropriate advice, without considering what others think. Another has the gift of giving good example. But each one is strictly obliged to uplift his neighbor by perfect example and by a holy and praiseworthy life.

These are the gifts, as well as many others, that are produced by love of neighbor. I made them so different that I could not give all of them to an individual man. To one, I allot this one gift, to another that one.

And yet, one gift can be had without the others because all the virtues are connected together. But there are many that are like leaders of the others. To one, I will give principally charity, to the other justice, to this one humility, to that one a lively faith, to this other one prudence, temperance, patience, and finally, to that last one, invincible strength.

All these numerous gifts, these benefits of virtues or other advantages, whether of body or of mind, are distributed in various ways. (When I speak of gifts in the corporeal order, it is a question of what is needed for the life of man.) If I spread them in such various ways, since I never give them all to the same individual, it is to oblige the exercise of charity one for the other.

I could well have furnished men with all they needed for the body and the soul. But I wished that one need the other and thus, they become my agents charged with distributing the gifts and graces they received from my goodness. Willy nilly, man cannot avoid the need to have recourse to charitable action in favor of the neighbor. And yet, if this action is not performed before my eyes, it will not obtain any profit of grace for him.

(Liturgy of the Hours proper to the Order of Preachers.)

Prayer to St. Martin de Porres

10. It Is the Living Man

O God, You Who have so gloriously lifted up the humble and so generously rewarded suffering and charity, look upon us, prostrate before You, and glorify your humble servant St. Martin de Porres.

And you, our blessed brother, glorified before the throne of the Lord, intercede for us, the poor and the humble, who are deserving of your compassion.

See to it that one day we will know the glory of heaven where you praise God in the company of the angels and the saints for all eternity.

Amen.

CHAPTER THREE

Some Cooperator Brothers of the Order of Friars Preachers:
- **Blessed Simon Ballachi (1250-1319)**
- **Blessed James of Ulm (1407-1491)**
- **St. Juan (John) Macias (1585-1645)**

"You have been called to freedom. Let not this freedom be a pretext to satisfy your egoism; on the contrary, place yourself in love to the service of one another. The entire law attains its perfection in a sole commandment, and this is it: You will love your neighbor as yourself. (See *Gal* 5:13-14.)

"What each of you has received as a gift of grace, place it in the service of others, as trustworthy agents of the grace of God in all its forms. If someone has the gift of speech, let him speak the Word of God. If he has the gift of service, let him fulfill it with the strength that God communicates. Thus, in everything, God will receive His glory through Jesus Christ." (See *1 Pt* 4:10-11)

1. Blessed Simon Ballachi (1250-1319)
Soldier, Vegetable Grower, Visionary

A strange adventure is that of this brother, born in the middle of the XIIIth century, whom history did not succeed in swallowing up in the multitude of the anonymous deceased. He was a native of Rimini. In the Middle Ages, this prosperous city of the Adriatic benefitted from a superb commercial position between Florence, Venice, and Byzantium. On these productive fields, wheat, fruit trees, onions, tomatoes, shared the with herds of cows the bounty of fertility. We do know that too much known abundance disturbs peace; cities become jealous of each other, and give themselves over to pretentious claims. Weapons and horse's hoofs rumble in the harvests.

What can an ordinary young man do in such a briefly described context? War and working the fields. Simon would do one then the other.

Still a young man we have to imagine him as a mercenary to the highest bidder. One after the other, he defended the Ghibeline partisans of the German emperor and the Guelfs, concerned with strengthening the power of the Pope-Lord in Italy. The brutality and the recklessness of the plunderer suited him for several years.

At age 27, he converted himself. The record does not indicate whether this was from hearing a word of the Gospel, a meeting, a wound, a killing more odious than the others. The mercenary was received at the Dominican convent in his city. He took the habit of a lay-brother and tended the kitchen-garden. For all that, the warrior did not die from his tool, he protected the vegetables from all harm. He carried with him the irons he imposed on his prisoners. For five Lenten periods, he fasted on bread and water up to the time his superiors asked him to interrupt this heroic practice. Our Italian brothers had never tasted the severity of Irish monks! Asceticism never makes a man more religious unless a very spiritual cry arises from physical compulsion. For Brother Simon it was our Father Dominic who gave meaning to these mortifications. Their apostolic goal remains in the conversion of infidels and sinners. Like Dominic, he prayed God with all his strength. He sighed, groaned, bent his knees, struck his breast, got prostrate on the ground, shed tears. He always required and asked of God more mercy and compassion for the world.

At the age of fifty-seven, he lost his sight. This was the time of his visions. The record speaks of his direct conversations with Jesus Christ, Mary, his mother, our brothers Dominic and Peter of Verona. He even hears: *Do not fear, Brother Simon, for you have found favor before God*. He was aware that this pacifying "do not fear" came from above him. In that XIVth century, fearing to see Satan reign through wars, sickness and misery, Simon resisted the noisy anguish and listened to his Lord. The blind man opposed his hardship with visions. Plunged into the night, he does not dwell on the punishment of God but rather on the pleasant conversation with Him..

This lay-brother with physical limitations entreated and implored with vigorous uninterrupted prayer the citizens of heaven. Offrédy, the city's physician, remained dumbfounded after having been healed by this know-nothing. The latter's reputation spread, petitioners came from everywhere. Some brothers admitted having been witnesses to wonderful events. Every time Simon prayed before the image painted by the evangelist St. John, a marvelous fragrance perfumed those present. It was a wonderful gift from heaven. If nothing else, the remembrance of this pleasant odor bears witness to the love he had for the evangelist and the joy that the community derived from it. The uproar rose at the doors of the convent, but the blessed Simon Ballachi was called to continue his life on a much higher and different plane. He died on 3 November1319.

In the streets of the city, long processions wailed for two days, in a last farewell to the inanimate body. The early faithful and visitors tore his habit into pieces. Since that time, he has received the respects of unending admiration. He rests in the collegiate church of St. Archan.

In 1817, the Church recognized him as Blessed in the sight of the world.

2. Blessed James of Ulm (1407-1491)- Stained-glass Maker, Mercenary, Fortunate Artist

James of Ulm wanted to become a stained-glass maker. In order to achieve this noble calling, he spent long years under the authority of a master workman who taught him methodically the techniques of grinding colors, melting, gathering, polishing, the skill of measuring quantities of silica, lime, oxide, acid ... secrets of transparency, the chemistry of shades that transform a humble sheet of glass into theological stained-glass. On this subject, James the German learned all that an artist had to know concerning the liturgy, from its symbolism to distinguish the martyr from the apostle or the doctor.

In Germany, the orders for stained glass were numerous — a rewarding career opened before him. The taste for adventure and the desire to perfect his trade pushed him onto the roads of Italy at his young age of twenty-five. In Rome, some Flemish and German artists received him; but among them, there were practically no glass men because in a country of light, the art of stained glass was little appreciated. Despite his disappointment, he was pleased with Italy. To supply for his needs, he enlisted as mercenary in service to Alphonsus V, king of Sicily. For four years, he participated in plunder and destruction. He deserted because of not having found better taste among his companions at arms, who seasoned their dish of cabbage with holy oil from a pillaged synagogue.

He settled in Capua, with a judge and consul whose property he managed. After five years of loyal service, he left to discover Bologna. On the way, he met some soldiers who pressed him to join the troops of Thomas Tartari. He entered a church to think things over, far from the noise, and found his calm restored near the tomb of St. Dominic.

A Dominican brother was walking in the nave of the conventual church. He was exercising the role of recruiter since James decided to engage himself for Christ and to consecrate himself totally to his service.

He was then thirty-four years old, his level of learning was sufficient for him to become a choir brother. But he chose instead the state of lay-brother. Hagiography explains to us that his virtue of humility led him to prefer this modest status. We can imagine another hypothesis: the lay-brother is one who does not follow a theological formation. James preferred to take up again the mechanical arts rather than to begin the studies required to become priest.

At Bologna, he learned artistic techniques, thus rounding out his craft as glass maker. Marquetry gave him more dexterity in adjusting panes of glass into the ribbons of lead.

The years of wandering were not unprofitable. His vagabond eye stored a vast collection of shades of colors; his heart overflowed with a thousand poetic subtleties suppressed during his military activities. His natural authority and his competence attracted disciples. With them, he formed a workshop that adorned with stained-glass windows the convent of Dominicans, the basilica of St. Petronius, the oratory of Blessed Helen in the Bentivoglio Palace. In this reviving Italy, he made his contribution to the renewal by finding the formula that led to a transparent yellow, thanks to the oxide of silver.

His contemporaries kept the memory of a devoted brother, always available and enthusiastic to insure the varied habitual services of the convent. His insistent meditation on the Passion of Christ, his very Germanic devotion to the crucifix, moved him to states of ecstasy. Some brothers bore witness to his face radiating light, like a sanctuary whose light comes from within. During his lifetime, and after his death, the Lord granted him the gift of miracles. The blind and those with dropsy more than others experienced the effects of his influence with the Lord.

He rests in the church of the convent of Bologna, beside our Father St. Dominic.

Pope Leo XII enrolled him in the catalogue of Blessed in 1825.

3. St. Juan (John) Macias (1585-1645) - Lay-brother of St. Magdalen Convent in Lima

Among the most important men who honored the Order of St. Dominic in the New World, John Macias holds an important place. The Church of Peru rightly claims him as one of its glories. With noble pride, it associates him in his veneration and homage to St. Rose of Lima and to St. Martin de Porres. Their altars are next to each other, and their names, confused in popular veneration, recall virtues carried to heroism, a brilliant holiness, and marvels of benefits that even in our day enrich those who invoke his name with faith and love.

Blessed John Macias was born in the year 1585, at Ribera, a city in the diocese of Valencia, in Spain, of noble but impoverished parents, due to a reversal of fortune in a state close to poverty. Pedro Sanchez, his father, and Agnes Sanchez, his mother, lived by the work of their hands. They placed all their care in raising their children in a holy manner, inspiring them with religious sentiments, with which they themselves were filled. John profited so well from this grace that he aroused the admiration of his surroundings by his modesty, his kindness, his diligence in visiting churches to pray or to hear the Word of God. From childhood, he showed marks of that eminent holiness to which the hand of the Lord was to raise him. His attraction for solitude was sharpened from day to day. Nothing equaled his animation in assembling in the cloisters of churches friends and contemporaries to pray together far from the noise or the gaze of men.

This child of blessing, that heaven was pleased to shower with special favors, received at the age of fourteen a significant gift. His patron, St. John the Evangelist, appeared to him in the form of a young man of stunning beauty, and promised that in future he would be his advocate with God, as well as his faithful protector in all encounters. Then, unveiling to his eyes the course of his life, he predicted that John would leave Spain, become a religious, and after his death, churches would be built in his honor.

Very early on, John had the pious custom that he would never abandon, of reciting each day three rosaries: one for himself, another for the conversion of sinners, the third for the souls in Purgatory.

The Christian education he received at home must have been for our Blessed and his brothers and sisters — very poor in goods of the earth — a heritage of highest value. Unfortunately, they were too soon deprived of it. John was not yet five years old when heaven, by taking away both mother and father, left him an orphan in the care of a paternal uncle. Unable to house him, the latter placed him with a villager, who, so John could earn his bread, had him keep watch over a small herd.

In this innocent country life, our young shepherd was no less solicitous to guard his heart as he did the sheep. On the hillsides, in the

Chapter Three

plain, along the edge of the woods, or on the shores of torrents, he fingered his beads without stopping, asking Mary to make known to him the holy will of God and to accomplish it. He received these insights that neither the knowledge of men, nor the flesh, nor blood can provide.

Having lived in this humble task for a large part of his youth, John Macias felt himself pressed interiorly to abandon everything and to attach himself exclusively to the service of the Lord, far from the trials and the scandals of the century. Without rushing things, he gave himself to prayer and fasting with renewed enthusiasm; then, no longer having any doubt about his vocation, he left for Seville. He had no support other than faith in providence and the protection of his heavenly Patron. The latter often favored him by his presence on the road, as the Blessed himself later declared to Father Gonzalez, his confessor.

The goal of the young man was to sail to America, where the spirit of God seemed to be calling him. Since he found no ship heading for this destination, he hurriedly left he capital of Andalusia, in fear of exposing his innocence to contact with a large city. He left for Xerez de la Frontera, a small town not far from Seville. This place became for him an earthly paradise; he found there all the spiritual joys that a soul, thirsty for solitude, finds in prayer. The church he preferred to attend was that of our convent. One day, while attending Mass, he was suddenly raised to deep contemplation. On studying the divine mysteries, he discovered so many marvels that, toward the end of his days, he admitted never having received graces comparable to these. On two occasions, he was honored with the same gift, without being able to control its effects.

Whatever care he took to live a hidden life, John Macias did not long remain unknown. His modesty, his enthusiasm, attracted the eyes of all onto him as on a friend of God. The Dominican religious, aware of his exercises of piety, uplifted by his long prayers and his frequent ecstasies, offered him to receive the habit. But it was not in Spain that he was to be clothed in it.

During his stay at Xeres de la Frontera, the virtuous young man profited from all his moments to be of service to others. He spoke little, prayed a lot, and did not shirk any good work. When he was not in church, he was certainly to be found at the bedside of persons either sick or in difficulty.

With the little money he earned from work with his hands, he was able to provide for his own needs, but also to relieve others poorer than himself.

By a sign from heaven, the Lord let him know the time he should leave for America. At San Lucas, John Macias boarded a ship bound for Cartagena, a city of New Granada. After forty days of sailing, he arrived safely in that city. His manner of life, during the crossing, impressed the passengers deeply. Indeed, many would have liked to have him in their employ.

The Vocation of Brother John Macias

But the man of God had other designs.

His final destination was Lima, and he had nine hundred leagues to travel before he got there. Poor as he was, he resolved to complete this arduous trip on foot.

It was not a minor undertaking to adventure alone through an immense territory, with no designated route, on which at every step the traveler risks being stopped, if not by Indians, at least by rivers, torrents, mountains, flooded moors, or impenetrable forests. John Macias had confidence in Divine Providence; his confidence was stronger than all the privations and dangers.

After a long trip of five or six months, he finally arrived at the capital of Lima, where God awaited him to make him the instrument of all manner of good works.

For about two years, he remained available and in service, awaiting the hour set by heaven to enter into a religious Order that would be indicated to him.

In a manner of speaking, he kept himself alert to grace; and when the appeal reached his ears, he did not hesitate to leave everything so as to request the habit of a lay-brother at the convent of the Magdalen. He was then thirty-seven years old. He employer was sorry to see him go. He fixed the price for his good services and, at the time of farewell, he added even more than he had promised, so moved was he by the feelings of this faithful servant who was leaving him only to give himself totally and definitively to God.

Once in the convent, the seriousness and modesty of John Macias, as well as his wisdom and his words, captivated all hearts. Father Salvador Ramirez, at the time Prior and later Provincial, quickly discovered that, under very humble appearances, the postulant hid a rare loftiness of feelings and perfect knowledge of the genuine maxims of the Gospel. Indeed, he received him gladly. It was on 25 January 1622 that taking the habit took place. The night that followed that beautiful day the happy Brother devoted to prayer, as much in gratitude for the benefit received as in requesting that interior spirit which alone assures the worth of religious acts. "Finding myself in this new status," said he one day, "I entreated the Lord to grant me the gifts and spirit of religion so as to place myself at his service with courage and enthusiasm, and be pleasing to him. At the same time, I asked my beloved Protector, St. John, not to abandon me. This he promised."

In entrusting the new religious to the hands of the Master of Novices, the Prior of the Magdalen did not lose sight of him. Quite the contrary, he liked to engage in conversation with him or to listen to him speak about the things of God. These conversations only increased his astonishment that an uneducated man was already so far advanced in interior paths. He had no trouble recognizing a privileged soul, endowed with all the gifts of the Holy Spirit and enriched with the most attractive virtues. In fact, our Blessed brother was advancing in giant steps on the road to perfection.

Every day marked for him some new progress. While he saw himself as the lowest in the house of the Lord, the most unworthy in the company of his brothers, the superiors proposed him to everyone as a model of religious life. We could never say enough about the joy with which he accepted the most humble tasks, his promptness in taking them up and the supernatural aspects they brought to mind. He was convinced, in fact, of the truth, too often ignored in practice, that all is noble in religion, and that the designated brothers should not seek a greater honor than that of serving their brother-priests, destined for the ministry of the altar and to the sublime functions of the apostolate. He was aware that the happiness of religious life consists in obeying, while ordinarily all sacrifice arises from the obligation to command. From this, the absolute deference for the slightest sign of an order; thence, respect, that filial confidence in holders of authority. Should we be surprised that, when seeing him carrying so nobly the banner of religion, the powers of hell soon armed themselves against him?

From then on, the struggles that Satan began against him were rude, varied, stubborn; but nothing was able to shake this soldier of Christ. The liveliness of his faith, the fervor of his prayers, his constant recourse to Our Lady of the Rosary, and his fidelity to the graces he received from heaven, made him victorious over the ancient serpent and all his wiles.

This is how John Macias lived during his first year of novitiate. The religious of the convent, fully convinced that this brother would one day be a great saint, agreed together to have him complete his solemn engagement only one year after his vestition on 25 January 1623. This decision was clearly in opposition to the tenor of the Constitution which required that lay-brothers lengthen their novitiate by three years before profession.

Nonetheless, the religious paid no attention to the reasons that called for such a wise rule and petitioned for a dispensation to confirm this choice of theirs.

On the very next day, John Macias was named assistant doorkeeper of the house, and shortly thereafter as official porter with the task of distributing and allotting alms. This task called for prudence, patience, and much kindness. The new incumbent held these dispositions so well that he was kept in this function the rest of his life. For twenty-four years, he fulfilled the duties and the services with utmost edification. In the juridical deposition required in view of canonization, the brothers were unanimous in declaring to the commissioners of His Holiness that he was the example for the whole community, a religious perfect on all counts, with no one ever being able to reproach him for having said or done, not even by a sign, even the slightest matter contrary to the perfection of his state.

This solemn deposition, in an act of such importance, summarizes the best vindication of the servant of God. But, in order to uplift us further in contact with his admirable virtues, allow us the satisfaction of examining them in detail, and to breathe their fragrance.

The Humility of Brother John Macias

Humility being the groundwork of perfection, our Blessed, who knew this, constantly worked at acquiring this virtue. Swallowed up in his nothingness, he considered himself as an unworthy man, covered in sins and in wretchedness. His words, his actions, his habits, his frugal nourishment expressed publically the feelings of his heart. It was very difficult to see his way of doing things without conceiving a sincere desire to imitate him. This disdain of self, which had nothing superficial or false, inspired at the same time an exalted idea of the neighbor. In his eyes, all his brothers were angels come down from heaven; thence, the modesty that startled in his relations with them. He treated everyone with a deep respect, manifested in his behavior, not only as regards his brother-priests and novices, but also towards all the brothers of the community. Kind toward religious and the most qualified persons of the city, the more he humbled himself before everyone, all the more were his merits extolled by an eager esteem and a kind of veneration that would become for this soul, so thoroughly humble and timid, the only anguish he had to dread. How often he was surprised hiding in some dark corner, to avoid being seen even by those who sought his prayers. Bewildered and mortified beyond expression, when some words of praise reached his ears, he had a difficult time holding himself back from stemming the words of his companion. The Lord, the sole witness to the anguish of his soul, spared him more than once from what he took as torment. Here is proof, The Marquis of Mantera, Viceroy of Peru, held the venerable Brother in high esteem, and never hid his feelings on this issue. The latter, who sought only to live and die an unknown like the patriarch of Idumea, suffered terribly from visits of this illustrious personage, whom he nonetheless received with his usual graciousness. One day when the Marquis came, once again seeking his holy friend, John Macias, John, having remained at the door, saw him enter but by a providential miracle the noble visitor, although right in front of him, did not see him. He was sought throughout the convent, called for, rung — a fruitless effort. John, quietly at his post, was seen by neither the viceroy nor the brothers engaged in looking for him.

The Prior, annoyed by the disappointment of the Marquis and thinking that brother had deliberately hidden himself, severely reprimanded the latter and obliged him to go in person to the palace of the viceroy to present his excuses.

John Macias answered modestly that he had always remained at his post. He had indeed seen the Marquis de Mantera enter and leave; but since the latter had never spoken to him, he himself kept a guarded prudence about him.

A similar incident took place with an audience of the royal house, who had come to the convent of the Magdalen to speak to the holy religious. Despite a most careful search, he could not be found. The realization came later that he had never left nor interrupted his duty as porter.

The patience of John Macias was no less remarkable than his humility. In the most disagreeable occasions, he seemed to lack sensitivity. Illness, afflictions, contempt, injuries: everything seemed to him immaterial. His face betrayed not the slightest sign of emotion, nor were there on his lips any word of complaint or resentment whatever.

An adolescent, called on occasion to shave the religious, began his service with Brother John. It was the first time that the young apprentice wielded the razor. While cutting brother's hair, he made deep gashes on his head. The blood flowed in several places. One religious happened by and stopped the barbarous execution. John Macias had uttered no complaint, nor did he sigh. When he was washed with fresh water, the cuts disappeared as if by miracle, giving place to a crown of rays that framed in a bright halo the head of the Blessed. Thus did God counterbalance the patience of his servant.

The Mortifications of Brother John Macias

But humility does not limit itself to inspire those persons it enriches with a sincere desire to humble themselves before God and men, or to carry with invincible courage the misfortunes and afflictions they undergo. It teaches them to see themselves as sacrificial victims, destined to appease divine anger at the price of great renunciation.

On this point, John Macias was one of the most illustrious penitents that heaven has given as example to the world in two centuries. He had chosen the convent of the Magdalen precisely because he knew that the religious of this community imitated very closely by their mortifications the life of the ancient Fathers of the desert. For all that, he was not content with ordinary practices. Clever in tormenting himself, he added to the use of a hair shirt and the metal belt frequent bloody whippings. Always ready to sacrifice himself, if only for the conversion of one sinner, he devoted his nights to prayer, shed abundant tears, fasted on bread and water, and did not spare any pain to obtain the deliverance of unfortunate slaves to sin.

Following the mortifications he practiced against his body, a wound appeared on his side that required a painful operation.

Once emerging from this unpleasant situation, the Blessed, far from diminishing his enthusiasm, armed himself with renewed courage and took up again his usual way of life.

He had overestimated his abilities. Weakened by the excess of his mortifications, barely able to stand up, he was to experience serious worries about health; at one point, he was believed to be about to die. The danger he risked agitated the entire city. A pious business man among friends approached him and could not stem his tears on approaching him. The esteemed sick person, more touched by the pain of his charitable visitor than by his own troubles, took his hand affectionately: "Be consoled," dear friend," he told him affectionately, "this small worm has not yet reached maturity."

The life of this man, who considered himself a little worm, was nonetheless precious to all the people. The Blessed quickly recovered and continued for several more years to render precious services to the needy.

There was nothing as angelic as the external behavior of this worthy child of St. Dominic. His usually lowered eyes never noticed his interlocutors. This modesty was becoming more noticeable when obedience obliged him to leave the convent or to speak with persons of the opposite sex. By this healthy precaution, the virtuous brother, so concerned about closing the entrance to deadly suggestions of the enemy, kept all his life an untainted purity. Two days before his death, he could declare to the Prior of the convent that, by a special gift, he was as pure and chaste as a child who was ignorant of evil. Besides, it was obvious, from time to time, to see shining on his face a particular reflection of the honesty of his soul.

Exposed to the most violent attacks, pursued for fourteen years by demons who oftentimes appeared to him visibly, weighed him down with temptations and left him unconscious, nonetheless the holy religious persevered in his religious exercises, pleased to suffer for love of God. He was no less pleased to see his patience and his struggles crowned with a modest victory. Later, he himself admitted to his confessor: "Often," said he, "Satan appeared to me in horrible guises, while I was praying. Since I remain immobile and firm in my prayer, my disdain irritated him all the more. Then he stamped his feet on me or threatened to strangle me. But my loving Savior delivered me from his anger. It was sufficient for me to say: 'Jesus, Mary, Joseph, come to my aid' to chase the enemy and put him to flight."

This perseverance in prayer was one of the distinctive traits of the virtue of our Blessed. Before his entrance into religious life, he devoted four or five hours day and night to prayer. Even then, the felt such strong emotions that twice, in our church at Xeres de la Fontera, his body carried away by the unpredictability of the spirit, was lifted up from the earth in the sight of those present. These gifts were more frequent in America. He was favored with them in every place he knelt down. Fathers Gonzalez Garcia and Louis de Espino were often witnesses to these raptures. The latter declared that, once, afer Matins, he saw Brother John rise up in the nave of the church, to such a height that he walked under his body and was unable to catch him by the hand.

A gift of prayer so sublime enriched the spiritual life of John Macias with eminent graces. He possessed the Christian virtues to the highest degree. His respect, his love for the Eucharist were the only pursuits of his heart. He never stopped investigating the mysteries of the love of Jesus Christ for men. The slightest irreverence in the holy place caused him genuine torment. It seems that his supernatural dispositions could have allowed him the privilege of daily Communion. Nonetheless, this gift was never granted: twice a week only was he able to approach the Holy Table. We can easily imagine the fervor with which he received the Bread of angels! In everything, our Blessed had no other rule than a blind and perfect submission to the voice of obedience. He accepted what was given him, and never asked for anything else.

From Jesus, he went to Mary; we dare to affirm that never did a son of St. Dominic show himself a more perfect imitator of the love of the blessed patriarch for the Virgin Mary. "It is a old custom," we read in the Bull of Beatification of the servant of God, "it is a pious custom of Holy Church to recall ceaselessly to the Christian people the memory of the important gift of the salvation of the world, and to furnish a two-fold food for the devotion of the faithful in those two sublime topics a God-man and a Mother of God. It was thus that all languages pronounced in unanimity the praises of such a Child and of such a Mother, and that all the churches of the world echoed happily the adorable names of Jesus and of Mary."

This is why Brother John Macias never wanted to separate the honor of the son and that of the Mother. The feelings of respectable affection that he showed for the Lord in His Sacrament he showed at the same time with filial tenderness to the Queen of Heaven, the Virgin Mary. This happened every night from eleven o'clock until dawn, when he remained in contemplation before a picture of Our Lady of the Holy Rosary that was honored above an altar where the Holy Sacrament was reserved. In this way, he spent the same amount of time in adoring the Son as in venerating the Mother. But day and night, with humble loyalty and inexpressible affection, he had recourse to Her who inspired in him the most complete confidence in her benevolent patronage.

Brother John Macias' Prayer of the Rosary

Faithful observer of the traditions of his Order, he practiced always with admirable enthusiasm the devotion of the rosary. According to the usage of the community, he ceaselessly wore a rosary around his neck, under the capuce, and held another in his hand to recite when an occasion arose. Almost never did he interrupt it even when serving in the refectory or when he assured the distribution of alms to needy persons. In all his manual labors, he recited the *Ave* incessantly, in such a way that, by this continual exercise, he ended up wearing out all the beads of his rosary. It was also a two-edge sword that he made constant use of to master the attacks of visible or invisible enemies, the very powerful shield by which he defended the innocence of his soul, finally, the banner of honor he wore up to his death. In his final hour, he asked Father Gonzalez Garcia to give to Don Juan, Count de Morroi, a man of solid piety, the rosary he wore at his neck; this was done, following his wish. This rosary, become a precious relic for having so long been in contact with this angelic body, was kept religiously in the de Morroi family, and remained with them as a kind of universal protection against all illnesses.

Moved by extraordinary fervor in his devotion to the Holy Virgin and the prayer of the rosary, our Blessed used all the means in his power so as to inspire love, as it had been practiced before him by our Father St. Dominic. He could never utter the name Mary without betraying a movement of indescribable tenderness. As much as he took care to decorate the church and the cloister for feast days and processions of the Blessed Sacrament, so much did he apply himself to embellish the altar and all the oratories of the convent on the solemnities of the Holy Virgin or for the processions of the first Sunday of each month. He

Chapter Three

liked also, on the second Sunday, to show his devotion and his ardent love for the Most Holy Name of Jesus, from which there resulted, clearly, that he could not honor the Name of the Son without honoring that of the Mother.

Thanks to his efforts and his zeal, the city of Lima decided to celebrate the feast of the sweet Name of Mary. By his warm entreaties, he was able to persuade His Excellency, Don Pedro of Toledo, and the Marquis of Manresa, viceroy of Peru, to provide a dowry for young impoverished girls, by giving to each girl one hundred fifty coins each worth eight *reals*.

John Macias acknowledged publicly that he was son and servant of the Queen of heaven: she was the one he approached for all his needs, from whom he requested advice in all confidence, before beginning a mission or a service. Accordingly, everything succeeded admirably.

Sometimes he prostrated in the chapel of the Rosary. One day while he was kneeling to pray, he felt attracted to the painting depicting the Assumption of Mary, placed over the altar. Thus suspended between the floor and the vault of the oratory, he remained a long time swallowed up in heavenly rapture.

A novice named Antonio de Spino, descending from the choir to pray in this chapel, saw the eyes of the Blessed in ecstasy; startled, he ran immediately to the door of the sacristy. The servant of God reached him and said: "Set your mind at rest, little angel; make no cry and do me the favor of not speaking to anyone before my death of what you have just seen happen."

In his room, John Macias had a painting on linen, representing the Holy Virgin in Bethlehem. It was especially before this portrait that, with naive simplicity he bared his soul in conversations filled with love. "Good Mother, you know very well that my poor persons will die of hunger, and I have nothing to relieve their misery; whom should I approach to remedy such great distress?" And the Queen of heaven used to answer him: "My child, ask this or that person; he will be generous for this mission." To the benefactors thus designated, Brother John would send a simple note in these terms: "Please offer a bit of bread for the needy." Immediately, abundant help was brought to him. These conversations with the Holy Virgin were frequently repeated every time the brother found himself in straits. He would address Mary and repeat his request: "O tender Mother, my poor have nothing to eat for tomorrow; I will send a note to such-and-such a family, no?" "Yes," responded Mary; "I will pray my Son to open the heart of this family to help you materially in your mission." Everything happened as foreseen. Thus, the advocate for the indigent never lacked for anything. But is was not only for unfortunate persons that John Macias consulted with Her in whom he had great confidence. He did the same for everything that personally touched him; every time, he was aware with certainty that Mary surrounded hin with a special protection.

Here is an example.

Before the ever growing iniquities of men, Our Lord allowed his arms to be weighed down, and willed, by a terrible earthquake, to show his justified wrath. The calamity plunged the city of Lima into extraordinary fear. It was night, at the time when the community was assembled in choir to chant the Office, while our Blessed, following his custom, was kneeling at the foot of the Rosary altar. At the first tremor, the terrified religious ran to the cloister. John Macias was about to do the same when Our Lady stopped him. Brother John, she told him, where are you going? "My dear Mother, I am fleeing with the others to escape from the severity of your divine Son."

"Return to your place; what are you afraid of? Am I not there for you?" The Blessed obeyed and quietly resumed his prayer, beseeching the august Queen of angels to have pity on the Christian people. The earthquake ceased at that very moment, and brother, lifting up his eyes, noticed that the painting was illuminated with heavenly brilliance. The entire chapel was flooded with it. After this marvel, the servant of God experienced in his soul a feeling of unspeakable joy and continued his prayer until morning. At dawn, he announced frankly that there could be no safer refuge against earthquakes than the chapel of the Rosary. The religious of the convent never forgot the memory of those words; every time a similar danger threatened, they took care to go to that chapel and to draw the faithful, telling them not to fear since Brother John had predicted they would always be safe.

The Love of God and of Neighbor

The goal of the love of God is to bring about and develop love of neighbor. On this score, our Blessed remains a model that the Church proposes to us. The rosary served him marvelously in the exercise of spiritual mercy regarding sinners to obtain their conversion, while his untiring charity suggested to him a thousand ways to provide for the material needs of persons in difficulty. We saw him entrust to his sweet Mother the interests of his dear dependants. The number of poor people he received was considerable, and no one left without carrying an offering or receiving especially needed urgent help. Time and again provisions multiplied in his hands.

Even though the religious never refused charity, whatever time of day someone came, he had nonetheless organized his general distribution at a fixed time in the morning: ten o'clock to noon. With that arrangement, he was placing a bit of order and judgment in his almsgiving allowing him to add nourishment for the soul to that of the body.

Two hundred poor persons surrounded him at the door of the convent and silently fell into place, women on one side, men on the other. As soon as the Blessed appeared, everyone knelt down and recited a short prayer with him, after which they received their food. This distribution of meals was followed by a thanksgiving prayer, a lesson, and a simple instruction on the duties of Christians. You can say that he had already created restaurants of the heart before Coluche in the XXth century. Since the heart of the servant of Jesus Christ was aflame with divine fire, his talk was among the most moving. He always ended by recommending a flight from sin, fear of the Lord, and confidence in his divine love.

To give an idea of the work of mercy and compassion that obedience enjoined on him, and at the same time to make known the resources that divine providence provided for his charity, it is enough to say that the reputation of John Macias, who was simply called "father of the poor," was not confined to the city or the province of Lima. The entire country resounded in the distance. Many persons who had never seen this brother sent to him from Quito, Potosì, Cuzco, and even Mexico, considerable sums to allow him to continue his works of charity. How many facts wherein miracles sparkled we would have to cite! One day, a young girl came to ask for a dress that she urgently needed. Brother John, taken unawares, hesitated for a moment, not knowing how to recover from his embarrassment, because he was loathe to send a poor person away empty-handed. "Wait a moment," said he, "while I go to my room." While running to the dormitory, he addressed a fervent prayer to God: "O ineffable goodness of the Host High regarding those who lovingly place their confidence in Him!" On entering his modest lodging, John Macias spied a package, set down by an invisible hand, that contained a new dress which he brought happily to the mendicant woman.

How many poor persons received a cure for their depression by sharing their meal with the holy brother who was giving it to them. But there is more. The Blessed knew by revelation the distress of those who did not dare to join the crowd of his visitors; it was especially for these persons wounded by life that his charity shown with greater brightness. The kindness of his behavior served to increase the value of his benevolent love. One could not even overlook an angelic intervention in the eager helps that always arrived at the right time, just as everything seemed to be lacking, without any word to hint of deep distress. These marvels, which recurred on a daily basis, had given to the porter at the Magdalen an almost irresistible influence on all hearts. But on occasion, there were some who remained hard-hearted and expressed proud disregard to his humble requests. On this score, these had nothing to be pleased about. A rich merchant in Lima, whom John had approached one day to obtain some cloth, would not hear of it and rather brusquely sent the Blessed away. This man was known as the top merchant of the City. From that day on, his business fell suddenly. Surprised by the unexplained change, he confided his trouble to a friend, while admitting to him that the unexpected reversal dated, so to speak, from the time when he refused alms to a Dominican brother. "Ah! My friend," replied his confidant briskly, "this brother whom you did not know is a saint; quickly send him what he wanted and you will see a change in your business." Effectively, as soon as he had given some money, the establishment recovered its reputation and took up in no time its ordinary way of operating.

Another business man was punished severely for his hardness of heart. He dealt in iron. One day, as he was embarking to take to Porto-Velo an enormous cargo of merchandise, John Macias approached him with a request for a modest sum to help needy persons. In spite of his entreaties, he was unable to get anything. It so happened that the cargo, caught at sea by a violent storm, foundered in the sight of the shores of Panama. Nonetheless, the life of the unfortunate merchant was spared and he returned to Lima in dejected sadness. This was the day after the death of our Blessed. The whole city rang with his praise and the renown of his miracles. Greatly moved by the stories, the merchant remembered the unjust refusal that he expressed, before his departure, to the discreet request of the religious. Filled with regret, he wished to repair his fault as soon as possible. He had delivered to the convent a sum greatly in excess what had been asked of his charity. That very day, he received word that part of his cargo had been recovered from the sea; this reduced his loss to less than half. [[Footnote concerning Louis of Granada omitted, p. 131.]]

The Fellowship of Heaven and Earth

The limitless charity that characterized the man of God did not end with his life. A number of persons called on him after his death and felt his protection in their distress. A widow, Antoinette Valdès, reduced to such want that she had no bread to feed her daughters, had recourse to the Blessed. "I know, good Brother Macias," she told him, "that you are now in heaven, united in that inexpressible charity that you longed for so much on earth. I believe, without the least doubt, that the plight of the poor is always in your heart. Take heed, then, I pray, of my request. To relieve my misfortune, I have only one chicken left to sell. Help me, you who were so prompt here below in comforting those who groaned in poverty." She recited then, in his honor, a *Pater* and an *Ave*. She had barely completed her prayer when two persons knocked on her door, one to give her a significant sum of money, the other to buy her chicken, for which she was willing to pay a good price.

The conversions, due to the intervention of the Blessed were as frequent as they were remarkable. It is not possible to relate all the events recorded by his contemporaries. Besides, one can find a record of them in the Bull of Beatification. Oftentimes, all it took was a word from him to open the hardest hearts. The following example will serve as proof. One day, the humble Brother saw enter the convent a man of distinguished appearance, who accompanied the Visitor General of the Royal Audience, de La Plata. After greeting them, John Macias gazed on the first, then took him by the arm, drew him to his lodge and showed him the crucifix. "My friend," said he "take a good look at your crucified Lord, and keep in your heart always the fear of God, and a great confidence in his love."

The Visitor de la Plata was strangely surprised at this scene, whose cause he could not explain to himself, knowing besides, that his companion was absolutely unknown to the Brother-doorkeeper. He felt a strange impression from this, while his friend left very moved, bewildered, and ran to the countryside to allow free flow to his tears. A few days later, he fell seriously ill, and had himself transported into the city; there, he declared that he was a miserable apostate. Having left a religious Order, after profession and reception of the diaconate, he had fled to the Indies where, having become captain of a vessel, he led a criminal life for a long time.

The words of the Blessed hit the target. Long against the goad, the sinner offered a heart docile to grace and died in admirable religious feelings, blessing and thanking him who had been the instrument of his salvation.

Regretfully, we omit a multitude of similar events, no less decisive. We will not judge the prophecies attributed to the Blessed nor his sudden apparitions, in spite of distant places, at the simple request of persons who had never seen him but who, on the belief in his reputation, had recourse to his intercession with respect and confidence. One such person, passing through Lima, thirty years after the death of John Macias, went to visit his grave. Learning the features of the deceased, he recognized the religious who earlier had appeared to him, and made a very significant deposition. Without a word, he had shown him where to find a precious object that had been sought for a long time; it had been believed that a housekeeper had taken it.

The Miracles of Brother John Macias

It is impossible to give a tally and an account of the miracles attributed to John Macias so numerous were they. Nonetheless, we cannot remain silent about one marvel the memory of which is perpetuated from generation to generation in the convent of the Magdalen.

During the construction of one of the wings of the convent, a carpenter having measured incorrectly, sawed a beam in such a way that it was one foot short for its intended use. One can imagine the despair of that workman: his blunder caused all work to stop; moreover, he lacked the lumber to cut another beam to replace the one that was no longer serviceable.

Brother John Macias visited the work site and saw this agitated man and inquired about the cause for his grief. "My friend," said John; "do not trouble yourself for so little" after having listened to him. "God is powerful enough to settle everything!"

Then he knelt on the beam and began to pray with fervor. When he got up, his face radiant, a significant miracle had just occurred. The beam, lengthening imperceptibly, finally reached the dimensions wanted. This extraordinary event had as witnesses all the workers employed for the construction.

The extraordinary favors with which heaven gratuitously enriched the humble religious, attracted to the convent enormous crowds of visitors. The name of Brother John was on everyone's lips, and without exaggeration, in all America. There was no important center where it was not greeted and praised like that of a saint. It was not surprising, then, that consternation became widespread when there was a threat of losing him who, in delight, was called father of the poor and of the orphans, the support of widows, the help and consolation of the sick, the shelter of all the needy.

For twenty-four years, John Macias had been wearing himself out in works of charity and in continuous prayer and mortification. His strength weakened; but, generous as always, he hid his sufferings carefully and did not spare himself in any way.

Towards the end of August 1645, he was stricken with powerful dysentery whose seriousness he immediately understood. Strong medicines were prescribed, that the patient accepted with docility, all the while declaring that his life was useless because he was reaching its end.

Appropriately alarmed, the religious of the community suggested that, for love the poor, he ought to ask of God for the lengthening of his days. John Macias responded: "Who am I that my presence be necessary in the interest of the good? God has need of no one to spread his blessings on whomever He chooses. Be convinced, Father Prior, that, after my death, the poor will continue to be assisted. Brother Dennis de Vilas is filled with charity for the afflicted members of Jesus Christ, and the donations will not diminish,"

Events proved that these last words, dictated out of humility, were a prophecy. Brother Dennis succeeded Brother Macias in his post as porter and dispenser of alms. He fulfilled this service with admirable enthusiasm. Providence always allowed him to respond abundantly to the needs of his many visitors.

During the three weeks he remained sick, John Macias found strength in his union with God and in the reception of the Holy Eucharist. His meditative mood was barely interrupted by the visits to which he had to submit.

The Marquis de Moncera, viceroy of Peru, and his son Don Antonio, subsequently viceroy of Mexico, wished to speak a few moments with the important servant of God. They left, transformed, and resolved to busy themselves seriously with their salvation.

CHAPTER THREE

The Death of Brother John Macias

On 16 September, the venerable patient asked to make his general confession and receive the last sacraments. That very evening, he told Doctor Corrasco, his physician, that on the following day he would be entering into eternal rest.

During the night, an enormous crowd, anxious for news, stood alongside the convent. Since the Blessed was visibly weakening, they prayers for the commendation of the soul were begun. Suddenly, his face lit up and appeared as bright as the sun. It was the hour to leave. Then, piously crossing his hands on his chest and fixing his gaze on heaven, John Macias gave up his spirit while saying these words: "In manus tuas Domine, commendo spiritum me." [Into your hands, Lord, I commend my spirit.]. He was in the sixtieth year of his life.

The bells had hardly announced his death that the people flocked to the conventual church. From everywhere there were only cries and groans. The crowd pressed around the holy body laid out in the choir of the sanctuary. Everyone wanted to touch him with a cross, medals, rosaries, and even, out of devotion, to snip some piece of his clothing. The funeral services of the humble Religious were among the most solemn, after which, the canons, royal auditors and the governor carried to the Chapter Room the body of the deceased in its cedar casket; it was marked with the seal of the city in the presence of the Archbishop of Lima and all representatives of official bodies.

A year later, the body of the Blessed, that was found to be perfectly preserved and always flexible, was taken to its former room. The religious had the favorable idea of transforming the place where John Macias formerly exercised his task as porter [i.e., receptionist] into a very elegant small chapel, with a choir, sacristy, and three altars magnificently decorated. Despite the precautions of the brothers of the Magdalen to restrain popular sentiment and prevent marks of exterior admiration — given the every increasing miracles that occurred at his newly glorious tomb — there was need to take note of evident facts and consider canonical procedures. Near the end of 1646, before the translation we have just mentioned, the Archbishop of Lima began the preliminaries of the process concerning the life and the miracles of the servant of God.

In 1659, the depositions were terminated. More than one hundred fifty witnesses had been heard. The documents collected constituted twenty-three volumes, which were sent to the Sacred Congregation of Rites. In the same year, the king of Spain wrote a very pressing letter to the Pope, requesting the beatification of John Macias. On 29 July 1660, he repeated his request and sent, for this purpose, an extraordinary ambassador to the Court of Rome.

The Archbishop of Lima, the University, the Chapter of the cathedral, the churches of the city: all had take the same steps in preceding years and addressed their petitions to the Sovereign Pontiff. On 15 October 1648, the Augustinians followed the example of the Franciscans, wrote a letter in the same vein. Finally, on 15 September, the religious of Mercy and those of the Company of Jesus joined their wishes and their entreaties to obtain for the servant of God the highest honors of the Church. Rome welcomed these diverse requests with lively satisfaction. The file was studied; when the heroic nature of the virtues was acknowledged, there followed the examination of the miracles, for which there was but an embarrassment of choice. Pope Gregory XVI placed his seal on the procedure by raising solemnly to the rank of the Blessed the humble lay- brother John Macias.

His liturgical office was granted to the entire Order of Friars Preachers as well as to the dioceses of Palencia in Spain and of Lima in Peru, who pride themselves, one for having given him birth, the other for having his tomb. This feast is celebrated on 18 September. On Sunday, 28 September 1975, His Holiness Pope Paul XI proceeded to the canonization of John Macias in Rome.

CHAPTER THREE

Prayer to St. John Macias

11. Perfect Charity

Lord, help us to bear with courage the weight of our daily work by following the example of St. John Macias, to whom you gave noble purity and perfect charity.

Through Jesus Christ, who lives and reigns forever.

Amen!

4. The Canonization of John Macias in Rome

An Eloquent Testimony for Evangelical Poverty

(Excerpt from the homily of Pope Paul VI at the process of canonization of St. John Macias).

John Macias is an eloquent and admirable witness evangelical poverty: the young orphan who with his modest pay as shepherd, helped the poor "his brothers", at the same time as he imparted to them his faith; — the immigrant in him, guided by his protector St. John the Evangelist, who did not seek riches, as did so many others, but that the will of God be fulfilled in him; — the innkeeper and the supervisor of grazing who secretly did not spare his charity in favor of the needy, even as they taught them how to pray; — the religious who made of his vows an exalted form of love for God and for the neighbor; who organized in his porter's lodge an intense life of prayer and mortification, the suitability of direct assistance, of distribution of goods to a veritable army of poor people; who deprived himself of a large portion of his own nourishment to give it to someone who was hungry, in whom his faith discovered the throbbing presence of Christ Jesus. In a word, is not the entire life of this "Father of the Poor", of orphans, of the unfortunate, a tangible demonstration of the fruitfulness of evangelical poverty, lived in all its fulness?

When we say that John Macias was poor, we are certainly not referring to a poverty — that God could not require or bless — a poverty equivalent to sinful misery or to an indolence unable to obtain appropriate well-being. No! We speak of that poverty, rich in dignity, that has to look for the humble bread of the earth as the result of personal activity. With what accuracy, what effectiveness did he give himself over to duties before becoming a religious as well as after! His patrons like his superiors gave enlightening testimony. It was always with his own hands that he sought to earn his own bread, bread for his brothers, bread for his multiple charities. This bread, the result of a socially creative and exemplary effort personalized, preserved, and configured to Christ, all the while filling the soul with confidence in the heavenly Father who feeds the birds of the air and clothes the lily of the fields, and who will not miss giving what is necessary to his sons. *Seek first the kingdom of God and his justice, and everything else will be added.*

On the other hand, the arduous task of John Macias did not distract his soul from the heavenly bread. He who, from tender childhood has been introduced to the intimate world of the presence of God, was always at the heart of his activity a contemplative soul. Nonetheless, this interior life never was for John Macias a flight from the problems of his brothers; quite the contrary, it led him from religious life to social life. His contact with God not only did not lead him to separate himself from men, but attracted him to them, to their needs, with more enthusiasm, more energy to help them, to direct them to a life more dignified, higher, more humane, more Christian. In this, he was only following the teachings and the wishes of the Church. With his predilection for the poor and his love for evangelical poverty, he never wished to leave them in their difficult condition but sought always to help them and to raise them up to always better levels of life, more in conformity with their dignity as men and sons of God.

Within these few, very limited traits there already appears to our eyes the marvelous and very attractive figure of our Saint. A figure of the present time. A bright example for us and for our society. In the course of his life, John Macias was able to honor poverty in two exemplary ways: with the confident search for bread for the poor, and the confident search for the bread of the poor, Christ who comforts everyone and leads to the transcendent goal. What a marvelous message for us, for our materialist world, often corrupted by a spirit of unbridled pleasure, by a deep social egoism! An eloquent example of that "interior unity" that the Christian has to achieve on his earthly task, imbued with faith and charity.

Evangelical Poverty

On Sunday, 28 September 1975, Paul VI proceeded with the canonization of John Macias, Here is the allocution he gave before the recitation of the Angelus in which he presented the new saint as an example of poverty for our time.

This morning, as you know, we have proclaimed as saint a Dominican lay-brother who died in Lima, Peru, in 1645: Juan (John) Macias. The principal characteristic of this new saint — a characteristic that he shares with other brothers in heaven and on earth — is the evangelical poverty that he practiced to an eminent degree in two ways, which themselves are constants in Catholic hagiography: detachment in the disposition of worldly goods, and lavishness in alms to the indigent who pressed at the door of the convent.

One could day that he was a man of another time. Yes, but he still has much to tell us and to teach us today. First of all, he reminds us more by his example than by his words that our life does not have, should not have as its principal goal the acquisition and possession of worldly goods. And yet, this is indeed the supreme end at the center of life for so many people, at the center of so many scientific, philosophic, and political opinions that dominate entirely the life of man of today, as if the possession of goods were what counted the most in our life. No doubt this possession is necessary, at least to a certain degree, but it is not everything. To be and to give are more important that to have. To be and to give as a good Christian should, it is wise and necessary to have the spirit of poverty, that is to say, to be detached from material goods and to subordinate them to the superior goods of the spirit, yes indeed as Christ teaches us in the kingdom of heaven. Poverty of spirit signifies deliverance, hope, fruitfulness. We should not forget this.

Accordingly, we would like this attitude toward worldly goods to make us able to use them not in an egoistic manner, but in a social manner. They become worthy of being pursued if they can also benefit others. Those to whom those goods are given become brothers because a link of mutual interest and affection that we call charity is created; this contributes something religious and even divine, even in our material life. Bread given in the name of Christ achieves this sublimation.

St. John Macias, humble doorkeeper at the convent of St. Magdalen in Lima teaches us this very humble and marvelous attitude that we need to imitate, even today, in so many new and efficacious guises, but with the same heart. The poor, Jesus told us, will always be with us. [Jn 12:8]

All of this we can learn by following the example of the new saint, and by enrolling in the school of the Holy Virgin.

The Message of John Macias

Conference of Father Vincent de Couesnongle, Master of the Order, on the occasion of the canonization of Bl. John Macias, given at Santa Sabina, Rome, on Tuesday, 30 September 1975.

John Macias did not preach; he did not write. This brother, now glorified before the entire Church, would be very astonished if he had been told then that his humble life would carry a message to the world, and more importantly, a social message. But it is precisely that humble life that today bears witness before us and constitutes this message.

John Macias was very young when he set out for the New World. He became an emigrant. He knew what uprooting was, a painful break with a very natural environment, with the tranquility of habits. He knew the leap into the unknown, the usual mixture of hopes and fears, the difficulties of emigration and adaptation. He was one of those millions of men who, for many centuries, were tossed from one country to another, not for their pleasure or for the taste of adventure, but because of need.

Without a doubt, this life of holiness, this life of love for the poor, he could have followed anywhere and at any time. But it was among that small group of uprooted persons that he became a saint, among the poorest. And that is what challenges us now.

Since the time of John Macias, the world has greatly changed. Not only have historical situations been profoundly modified, but thanks to a clearer reading of the Gospel — and, we must admit, under the pressure of events — the Christian people have opened themselves to wider demands for charity. It has been understood better that charity cannot be reduced to some individual gestures of kindness, of attentiveness, or even of heroic individual sacrifices in the service of others. It has been understood that charity has to animate, take over and transform all sectors of the life of men and of the organization of human society.

Fraternal charity is not a gratuitous luxury to be indulged in by those who have time, the money, or the inclination. Fraternal charity is not simply a benevolent compensation to remedy the deficiencies of a social order that crushes the poor.

To be sure, compensations will always be needed. But the first requirement of charity is justice for everyone. It is the most famous statement of one of our predecessors, Father Gillet: "The charity of today has to become the justice of tomorrow." To love one's brothers is above all to have them admitted to our world, to our society, as full members. It is to wish by effective and concrete means that they feel themselves recognized, welcomed, accepted in their dignity as man.

True charity requires that we work, to the full extent of our possibilities and responsibilities, for the building up of a more just, more humane, more fraternal society.

We add, nonetheless, that a world perfectly just, with perfect laws, and in which the rights of each one are assured, could still be a cold world, without soul, without hope if it is without love. Justice alone can be inhumane, and no public law can give rise to charity. A disciple of the Gospel must be particularly sensitive to this aspect. Christians are called to build a just world wherein the relationships between men, between peoples, between diverse communities, be relationships of love. This is the message of the Gospel. This is the message of Brother John.

In fact, it is more than just a message because it is something other than a kind of testament or posthumous lesson. It is the shock of a new look on the world, it is the impulse of a leap of the heart, it is a leaven, a source of flowing life.

Moreover, the message of John Macias is not simply social. Above all, it is a theological message. By opening our eyes to the *opera bona* [good works] accomplished by John Macias, the Church invites the Christian world to *glorify our Father who is in heaven*. And this, by shedding more light on one aspect of the name and the face of God. By his charity towards the poor, John Macias manifested the true name of God to the Indians of his time who did not know Him: God is love.

JACQUES AMBEC OP: ST. MARTIN DE PORRES

APPENDICES

- History and Phraseology of the Word:"Lay-Brother" to "Cooperator Brother."
- The Cooperator Brother Today
- The Proclamation of the Gospel of Life

The mission of the Order of Friars Preachers and the form of its brotherly fellowship determine the character of the religious society. Since the service of the word and of the sacraments of faith is a priestly office, the Order remains a clerical-type association whose cooperator brothers — who exercise in a special manner the common priesthood — share also in the mission in multiple ways. On the other hand, solemn profession which binds in everything and for always each preacher to the life and mission of Christ, manifests that he is completely deputized to the proclamation of the Gospel by word and by example.

[From the Book of Constitutions and Ordinations of the Friars Preachers]

1. History and Phraseology of the Word: "Lay-brother" to "Cooperator Brother"

How appropriate is it to call the brothers, lay members of a religious congregation of clerics: lay-brothers coadjutor brothers, servant brothers, cooperator brothers or auxiliaries, missionary brothers? In the history of religious life, all these terms have been used interchangeably.

First, they were called converts, which is to say, those who have separated themselves from the world or are in the cloister. Are not all the baptized also invited to separate themselves from the world to follow in separation the evangelical counsels? To convert oneself, to turn to God and the service of the Lord meant about the same current reality "to enter religion." Monks were "converts." Following the slow evolution of history, the name was reserved to monastic orders (Benedictines, Cistertians, Carthusians, Camaldolese), to those who worked the lands of the abbey or of the monastery and maintained external relationships, thus protecting the cloister of the monks and allowing them to accomplish in peace and serenity the service of prayer as required by the liturgical life of the community.

In the apostolic orders of the XIIIth century, the mendicant orders (Carmelites, Dominicans, Franciscans, Servites), convert brothers assured the material services in the interior of the convents to allow the brothers-priests free and complete exercise of their ministry outside the community. Mendicant religious had forsworn the exploitation of large properties. These two types of brothers in a monastic Order and in the mendicant Orders, commonly identified by the same name, were already very different one from the other.

Froin the XVIth century on, the Orders and the Congregations founded to answer to the needs of new times, gave another style of life to their brothers who were no longer called "converts" but "coadjutors." In fact, these priestly religious families continued to associate lay persons to their mission of evangelization. Nonetheless, these laymen remained coadjutor brothers entrusted with material tasks, even if their founder had clearly foreseen for them a more active participation in the apostolic service of the congregation; they took only an indirect part in the apostolate. This was the case with the Jesuits, the Lazarists, the Oblates of Mary Immaculate, the Spiritans, for example.

In our days, the separation between clerics and brothers in the same institute tends to be minimized. Are not priests and lay men religious under the same title since they pronounce the same vows and follow in common the same ideal of evangelical life? The brothers are cooperators in the apostolic ministry. Many congregations, even recent ones, have kept the name auxiliaries: Auxiliary Brothers of the Missionary Brothers of Country Towns, Auxiliaries of the Clergy. It appears that this designation is not the best and does not express in a satisfactory way the status and the mission of the brothers in today's settings. The word "auxiliary" too strongly evokes an exterior contribution and a secondary service. In the Order of Friars Preachers, we are keeping the designation "cooperator" which expresses the reality better and which has the advantage of being a biblical term. The Church at Philippi had sent the Christian Epaphrodi, "that brother who is my companion in work and struggle and whom you delegated to help in my need." [See *Phil* 2:25]. In the qualifier "cooperator" there is no distinction of lesser dignity, but a pure and simple indication of community of work and of service for Christ.

Nonetheless, it has become current to speak today very simply of "brothers." In a monastic Order can be found priests and brothers; the ones and the others are monks. In the apostolic Orders, we find priests and brothers who cooperate in diverse ways in the same apostolic ministry for the conversion the salvation of the world and the proclamation of the Good News.

And yet, this appellation has not definitively been fixed. New events and new developments could bring about another change.

Comments from Cooperator Brothers

During the year 1998, the provinces of France organized an inquiry and a study among all the cooperator brothers to ascertain their opinions about this adjective: *cooperator*. Should it be preserved, or rather, should another designation be sought? By a strong majority, the brothers answered that they hoped to keep this definition and to be called "cooperator brothers." The terms "brother not priest" and "non-ordained brother," or simply "brother," were not retained nor proposed.

The key ideas gleaned after the scrutiny of the questionnaire sent to all the cooperator brothers of France are summarized as follows:

1. The cooperator brothers place themselves at the service of the community to remember our universal and unique calling; all of us are servants — to announce the word of God and first, to live it together. (Brother Jean-François)

2. It is a question of living every day the fraternity that, according to the Gospel, implies mutual respect in sharing and *complementarity*. (Brother Dominique Richard)

3. Cooperator brothers maintain the sign of a fully lay life, lived in a family of clerics. (Brother Gérard-Marie)

4. For his manual or more material labor, the cooperator brother places himself at the service of the community so that the brothers-priests be more available for preaching, teaching, and communicating the Word of God. – One brother added a precision: to hear confessions, the ministry of reconciliation, linked to the concern of St. Dominic for the service of mercy and compassion. (Brother Thomas)

5. There is no prototype for the cooperator brother. Some will have professional work whether in associations or will concern themselves with liturgy or the arts, others surely in material tasks in the convents. Each one will find his place in the Order according to his personality and his dispositions so that his vocation be fully realized. (Brother Jacques B.)

6. Every brother can fulfill completely his Dominican project within the community in services that are indispensable: like reception, the management of goods, concern for the poor and the sick through using human dispositions that do not require priestly ordination, but on the contrary, a preparation and progress in sacramental life. (Brother Jacques A.)

7. The relationship between clerical brother and cooperator brother that so often has brought about misunderstandings and suffering, to my mind, arises from a lack of human formation, spiritual, intellectual, and professional; from an anachronistic division of work and the sharing of indispensable tasks for the effective workings of the

common life, from an unadmitted wish by many brothers to be served at lower cost and to forego willingly certain services, deemed indispensable, so that the community function normally. (Brother Louis-Marie)

Words of the General Chapter of Kraków [footnote omitted]

From the very beginning, St. Dominic incorporated in his apostolic task the presence and the work of brothers who, without being priests, contributed to Holy Preaching, accepting obedience and cooperating according to their abilities in the daily needs of brothers and of convents. This calling is maintained in the Order by the service of numerous brothers cooperators who, consecrated to the service of preaching, contribute to the apostolic diversity of the Order. [Kraków, 2004, Common life, #10]

2. The Cooperator Brother Today

The fundamental Constitution, in #VI, explains: *Since the service of the word and of the sacraments of faith is a priestly one, the Order is a clerical organization whose cooperator brothers, who exercise in a special way the common priesthood, also share in the mission, in multiple ways.* From this, we can extract two characteristics in the life of the brothers: similarity and complementarity. *Similarity*, because the cooperator brothers share in the same status of religious as the brothers-priests. They wear the same habit, join in the same prayers, and participate in the same internal obligations (but the cooperator brother cannot be elected prior). It is religious profession that admits us into the Order. We pronounce the same vows. We all choose first to be religious; most will become priests to answer to a call from the Order, so as to assure this or that ministry. *Complementarity* because the cooperator brothers fulfill tasks that aid, make it easier, develop and complete the mission of the brothers-priests. More and more they are assuming the administration of Dominican houses: purchasing, the sacristy, receiving guests, the library, the clothes closet, sometimes even the kitchen, thereby freeing other brothers for study and apostolic work. They receive at the receptionist post those who knock on our door. This is an important service: for our visitors, the cooperators are often the brothers of first contact, the first Dominican image. One gesture, a simple word will bring the understanding that religious life is not what uninformed persons could imagine about conventual life.

The complementarity of the cooperator Brothers will no doubt assume new and unexpected, forms in future years. Some of them have already assumed responsibility for health services: General Director of the Hospitality of the Rosary, hospital chaplain, agent for association of AIDS patients with ministry of health. Some cooperator brothers in Canada are involved in the area of culture, others in the United States as professors, some remain in parochial work and insure teaching catechism in Italy and Spain, others have chosen professional activity. It is true that it is no longer necessary to be a priest in order to engage in preaching in all social environments. The typical picture of the cooperator brother has become blurred. The pathways increase in number. The future is a matter of freedom of choice and imagination.

At this time, Dominican religious priests and brothers number 6,500 in the world, spread in 83 provinces. France accounts for 630 religious, of whom 23 are cooperator brothers (2004).

For the multiple needs of service and the influence of our community, these numbers remain very insufficient. In France, at this time, some convents do not have any cooperator brothers among religious members. This is a shortcoming and a felt gap, not only to insure indispensable domestic tasks but also to preserve the quality of fraternal life in our communities. Moreover, one prior has called the cooperator brothers "these indispensables."

Perhaps there is further need to make known the existence, the usefulness, and the reasons for this attractive Dominican vocation that shares completely in the mission of the Order of Preachers as intended by St. Dominic: holy preaching. It is the entire community that preaches, that announces the Word of God, even in the most humble responsibilities, in the silence and the discretion that the cooperator brothers often take upon themselves in communities.

St. Martin de Porres as well as St. John Macias remain for us models of that calling. We can ask them by our prayers to send us vocations to the cooperator brothers.

Prayer to St. Martin de Porres

12. Prayer for Vocations

> Merciful God you have given us through St. Martin de Porres a perfect model of humility and of charity. You, O God, saw in him his fidelity and not his status and have glorified him in your Kingdom while the chorus of

angels sang. Look upon us with compassion and give us an appreciation of his powerful intercession. Provide us with generous men who, following our Father St. Dominic and like St. Martin de Porres, wish to live wholeheartedly this religious life in humble service to our communities to insure the proclamation of the Gospel.

Obtain for us vocations to the cooperator brotherhood and spread among us the benefits of your noble charity; intercede on our behalf with Our Lord who has so well rewarded your merit in eternal glory.

Amen.

The Varied Tasks of a Convent

For many years now, I have taken on the responsibility of reception at the door of the convent in Toulouse with the collaboration of a team of devoted volunteer laymen, among whom two belong to lay Dominican fraternities.

In the XIIIth century, Humbert de Romans said of the qualities of the doorkeeper: "the watch at the door is to be entrusted to a brother of mature age, of agreeable manner in receiving, who disturbs no one by the harshness of his responses, who knows how to calm down worried visitors."

In the course of time, I have calculated how much patience and care were needed to listen to the requests and the questions of visitors and of speakers on the telephone so as to meet and respond to the diverse requests.

Occasionally, the person in great distress or in need has to be directed to appropriate and effective places of reception and social help to resolve problems of housing, employment, and urgent assistance. On principle, we do not give any money but I will prepare a sandwich for the person who would like one. The quality of our welcome is summed up in an attentive listening to the person seeking material, as much as moral and spiritual, help. What brother will I call to satisfy this person who seeks a meeting? I often think of the words of Mother Teresa: "Never receive anyone without having him be better and happier when he leaves you." I believe that these words encapsulate our mission.

The door service remains a school of patient charity that gives an exact picture of the entire life of the convent, of the relationships and of the tasks that the brothers fulfill according to their diverse activities whether in the interior or the exterior of the community. Accordingly, to be sure, we need to be vigilant and discreet: "I know. I see. I hear, but I say nothing."

Actually, the cooperator brothers receive a solid formation, human, theological, spiritual and professional, so that they may be able to exercise responsibilities for tasks that are indispensable for proper functioning of the common and fraternal life of our communities. I think of the brothers who manage the linens, care for clothing, make religious habits and other dry goods needed for life together. A cooperator brother is assistant librarian at the convent of Toulouse.

Other religious, not priests, are in charge of the infirmary and of management. At the convent of St. Thomas Aquinas, one cooperator brother, in collaboration with lay persons, has the heavy and forbidding burden of economic matters for the convent of Toulouse and the handling of all economic questions — such as our Father St. Dominic wanted it at the beginning of the XIIIth century.

In many convents around the world, some cooperator brothers fill the task of welcoming at the entrance as did in Lima Brothers Martin and John Macias who held this very important function.

The doorkeeper receives and informs all those who come to the convent. He is not only a benevolent guardian but also a messenger, an agent of communication, a link between people on the outside and the religious of his convent. He reflects the mind set, the spirit, the face, and the religious attitude of his community, whose living witness he remains.

I am more and more convinced that it is through this service of welcoming that needs to be shown the extensive mission of our Dominican calling — namely, to testify to the mercy we requested at the beginning of our religious life, and that the compassion we manifest by many gestures of love, of goodwill, of gentleness, may make visible. "It is by the love you have for one another that you will be recognized as disciples of Christ."

Dominic founded the Order of Preachers so that, throughout the world, there be multiplied "sanctuaries of compassion." These sanctuaries of compassion are formed by men who, like Dominic de Guzman, Martin de Porres, John Macias, and so many others in their wake, allow themselves to be touched, grasped, and transformed by the love of God for their neighbor.

Assuredly, are not all our communities called to be or to become places and signs of a concrete manifestation of that compassion for our sisters and brothers in need?

Prayer of Welcome

13. With a Smile

>A smile costs nothing but produces a lot.
>It enriches those who receive it,
>Without impoverishing those who give it.
>It lasts but a moment,
>But its memory is sometimes eternal.
>No one is that rich that he can do without it,
>No one is that poor as not to deserve it.
>It creates happiness at home, soothes things over.
>It is the tangible sign of friendship.
>A smile gives rest to a tired being,
>Gives courage to the most discouraged.
>It can neither be bought, loaned, or stolen,
>Because it is something having no value

Except at the moment when it is given.
If sometime you meet such a person,
Who no longer knows he has a smile,
Be generous, give him yours,
Because no one has so much need of a smile
Than he who cannot give one to others.

One day, on receiving a group of American researchers, the religious of Kolkata, Mother Teresa, greeted them with these words: "Smile to your neighbor; take time for the members of your family; smile to all of them. We will never know the good that can be accomplished with a simple smile."

APPENDICES

Prayer to St. Martin de Porres

14. Daily Prayer

"Courage, good and faithful servant; because you were faithful in small things, I will set you over greater ones." [See *Mt* 25:21]

St. Martin de Porres pray for us.

That we may be worthy of the promises of Jesus Christ.

St. Martin de Porres, fire our hearts with that ardent charity that made of you the consoler of your needy brothers and the protector of animals.

Now that you are in heaven, your are more powerful than you were on earth; do not abandon us! Hear the supplications of your needy brothers.

Protect us against the misdeeds of destructive animals. Grant us to imitate your virtues so that by your example, we may know how to accept the state of life and the conditions of being in which God has placed us! May we too carry our cross with strength and courage! On the painful way, may we always follow in the serenity of Our Savior carrying his cross!

In your footsteps, may we too attain the heavenly Kingdom, through the merits of Our Lord Jesus Christ, who lives and reigns for ever. Amen.

3. The Proclamation of the Gospel of Life

For us preachers, all our words have value. Each word can offer life to others, or death. The vocation of all members of the Dominican family continues to offer words and accomplish signs that give life and speak of it. From evening to morning, we refresh each other with words; we jest, we exchange information, we speak about the absent. Do these words bring life, or death? Healing, deliverance, or on the contrary, do they favor rejection, exclusion?

One of the mottos of the Order is to praise, to bless, to preach, to glorify. To become a preacher, it is very advantageous to speak about God. It is the discovery of the art of glorifying and blessing all that reflects goodness as much as beauty. There can be no preaching without celebration. We cannot preach if we do not glorify, if we do not bless the marvels that God manifests for each one of us in his life. The preacher must sometimes, like Las Casas, confront and denounce injustice, but only for the sole purpose of having life win over death, of resurrection over the grave, of glorification over accusation. We could call upon this unending struggle to break the silence that exists in the face of AIDS in the populations of Africa: "no to the AIDS of the poor." The absence of effective prevention that resists the traditions of diverse ethnic groups and the difficulty of access to care make of it a plague for all those countries on the way to development, that cannot obtain treatment except at too high cost for them. Yes, the rich countries of the North where are found 95% of the medicine ought to help the poor countries of the South with its 95% of the sick, namely, more than 30 million persons stricken in 2004. An urgent challenge is asked of us; a struggle of life in the face of death to rebuke this scandal which reminds us that we are all invited to a sharing and to solidarity. "God did not create poverty," Mother Teresa said in 1990; "we are the ones who create it because we do not share." And the holy one of Kolkata gave a concrete answer in the practical counsels she lived every day with her sisters.

"We cannot be satisfied to give money, because it can be acquired. It is from our hands that the poor need to be served, it is from our hearts that they need to be loved. The religion of Christ is love, the contagion of love." *(Mother Teresa)*

Escorting: a Presence of Love

Our escorting structure *SELF: SIDA, Espérance, Lumière et Foi* (AIDS, Hope, Light, Faith) was born [set up] in Toulouse in September 1996 to fulfill the many needs of persons contaminated with the AIDS, who are too often alone, isolated, rejected, excluded because they are unable to live a normal life. Even today, they remain dependent on diverse onerous and alarming treatments. We respond to the demands, to the appeals and the various needs that appear so as to give to those HIV or ill patients a presence, a hearing, a sharing of tenderness and love, a path of spiritual escorting with the strength and support of prayer for the persons who are seeking.

Christine, a patient, confided to me: "I am as if married to this damned virus that from now on leads my life and plunges me into terrible anguish for fear of setbacks, of returning to the hospital, of migraines, or of digestive difficulties brought about by the medicine that I will have to take up to the end of my life."

Our structure is flexible enough to resolve the human needs of the person touched by AIDS so that he (or she) be surrounded, respected, taken into consideration, loved, and thereby find again his dignity as well as to accompany the spiritual steps that always show up at a certain stage of this illness.

Thus do we honor the invitation of Jesus to live that beatitude of compassion: "Lord, the one whom you love is ill." [*Jn* 11:3] Or again: "I was sick and you visited me... In truth, I tell you, to the degree that you have done this for one of the least of my brothers, you did it for me." [See *Mt* 31:35 seq.]

APPENDICES

St. Martin de Porres, as much as St. John Macias, stirs us through the testimony of his life and his holiness to continue this struggle in favor of life.

The prayer of Bruno

15. For a Visit to a Sick Person

> You who will come to see me, do not forget that you remain my hope.
>
> If you come out of pity, do not forget that I asked nothing of you.
>
> If you come out of curiosity, do not forget that death is not a plaything.
>
> If you come out of compassion, do not forget that I seek only your affection.
>
> If you come to judge me, do not forget that I am already condemned.
>
> If you come to weep, do not forget that all my tears have been spilled.
>
> But if you come to escort me, then your coming will be welcome.

This poem was left by Bruno as a testament before his death in Toulouse in 1996, following upon AIDS. It was read at his funeral obsequies.

Escorting: The Influence of Prayer

In May 1994, after the death of Jacques [footnote omitted], one of my precious friends whom I escorted up to the passage of death, the first prayer group was established at Blagnac. The influence of prayer of SELF resides in this team of prayer placed under the patronage of St. Dominic. The act of listening as much as of praying allowed us to hear the cries and the resistance of persons who were suffering. Prayer remained the power to escort these sick persons in this humanly very difficult step. Suffering can lead to growth. It is one of the possible paths of patience that lifts us up in faith if on the way we meet a compassionate person, a Simon of Cyrene, a Samaritan like the one in the parable of the Gospel by the same name. [See *Lk* 10:30-37]

The testimony of the Christian must simultaneously be concrete and spiritual. It is not sufficient to say: *Lord, Lord*, but one must go the end, up to being at the end of one's tether in the sharing of that intense sorrow that floods our brothers. This is communicated by trivial gestures, by word as much as by silence, but always with the power of prayer. The entire Dominican family is concerned by this mission – brothers, sisters, and lay Dominican fraternities.

Numerous sick persons have told me: "I need your prayers." I have always answered "Likewise." We need to pray together to the degree that the patient is able.

Indeed, I tell you the truth; if two of you on earth join voices to ask anything of me, it will be granted by my Father is heaven. [See *Mt* 18:19]

I always use the defensive weapons of love, of patience, and of prayer. These dispositions of the heart I find necessary and complementary at the bedside of a sick person to accompany him in his painful and delicate condition, as well as for the greater service that can be given to anyone, to love him. Remember the words of the Gospel: "Lord, the one you love is ill."

Prayer is contagious, but is not dangerous; it is not a sickness. Since the year 2000, there exists a second prayer group in Toulouse, one that carries the name of St. Martin de Porres. Now we know better how his spiritual life and his encounter with the Lord developed and stimulated his charity towards his neighbor just as it did our Father St. Dominic — which explains the choice of names for the prayer groups.

The **St. Dominic Group**, at the home of Marie Dupon in Blagnac [tel.: 0561 71 26 74]

The **St. Martin de Porres Group**, at the home of Mr. & Mrs. Faure in Toulouse [tel.: 0561 80 88 48]

Escorting: The Sharing of Generosity

In 2004, throughout the world, every ten seconds one person died as a consequence of AIDS. The virus continues its spread. In Africa, more than 26 million persons are known to be contaminated. The situation in Asia is becoming worrisome. India, China, and Cambodia are the three most affected countries. In Europe, it has proven impossible to control and to stabilize this pandemic. The treatments are more troublesome for sick persons; consequently, escorting requires more frequent presence, listening, and support during the extent of the care, the anguish, the discouragement, and even some difficult moments that give rise to depression. This requires a strong relationship based on confidence, friendship, sharing...

• In our SELF structure, we were able to participate financially in the operation of the dispensary of Dzobegan, in Togo, that welcomes and treats ill persons. This monastery is a foundation of the Abbey of En-Calcart in the Tarn [region in France] that assures the administration for the shipment of goods through an intermediary association: the AAFOD [Association of Friends of the Foundation of Dzobegan, in Togo].
En-Calcat: 81100 Dourgne.

- Through the intermediary of the foundation of friends of Mother Teresa in Paris [contact omitted], we are able to contribute to the welcome and the services for persons with AIDS, whom the missionary sisters receive in their *House of Love*, in Nairobi, Kenya. At no cost to themselves, the sick come to receive services, along with the consideration of love, and for many, to die with newly-found respect and dignity. In that country, are recorded more than 3 million persons contaminated with HIV in a population of 30 million.

- We are sponsors of Samuel, a teacher in Tanzania and finance his treatment totally at 2102 € per year.

For donations ... [addresses omitted]

Escorting: In the Face of AIDS, Prevention and Information

On 30 September 2004, in Rome, Pope [St.] John Paul II published a letter for the XIIIth World Day for the sick which was to take place in Cameroun on 11 February 2005, at the Sanctuary of Yaounde, dedicate to Mary, Queen of Apostles.

If the objective of these days is to stimulate reflexion on the notion of health — which in its full extent also alludes to the situation of harmony between the human being within himself and with the surrounding world — this is precisely the vision that Africa expresses richly in its cultural tradition. Unfortunately, this harmony remains greatly disturbed today. Among the many illnesses that devastate this continent, in particular the scourge of AIDS, conflicts and wars, we must add also those who are responsible for the sale of weapons.

"The attention of the Church to the problems of Africa is not motivated only by philanthropic compassion, but also by compliance with Christ the Savior whose features we recognize in those of each suffering person. It is faith, then, that impels her to become involved in the care of the sick, as she has always done in the course of history. It is hope that makes possible her perseverance in that mission, whatever obstacles of various kinds she may face. Finally, it is charity that suggests the proper approach to diverse situations, allowing her to be aware of the particularities of each and to correspond accordingly."

This is also the opportunity to explain the position of the Church in the face of a drama, for which she is often accused.

In the first of this letter, the Pope brought up the question of prevention:

"To combat AIDS in a responsible manner, one must increase prevention by education for the respect of the sacred value of life and by the formation and the presence of a correct practice of sexuality. If the contagious infections through blood are numerous, notably in the case of pregnancy — infections that will be fought vigorously — more numerous are those that arise from sexual ways, that can be avoided, especially thanks to responsible behavior and the observance of abstinence or the virtue of chastity."

Moreover, he reminds the bishops of the recommendations of the 1995 synod for Africa in the face of "the incidence of irresponsible sexual behaviors in the spread of the illness... the affection, joy, happiness and peace arising from Christian marriage and faithfulness, as well as the security given by chastity, must continually be presented to the faithful, especially to youth."

The followup of this message concerns the struggle against AIDS in which "everyone must feel himself involved, even the Church herself. Administrators and civil authorities must provide clear and correct information for the benefit of citizens and deliver sufficient details for the education of the young and satisfy all the needs of the sick.

The Pope encouraged all the international organizations concerned to promote in this domain initiatives inspired by wisdom and solidarity, looking always to the defense of human dignity and to the protection of the inviolable right to life. He hailed and praised with conviction the pharmaceutical industries who bound themselves to maintain at a just price the cost of medicine useful for the treatment of

AIDS. The safeguarding of human life must precede any other evaluation.

Returning to the apostolic exhortation *Ecclesia in Africa*, John Paul II insisted that pastoral workers carry to their brothers and sisters afflicted by AIDS all the comfort and relief possible, whether material, moral, or spiritual. He then turned with admiration to the numerous volunteer health workers, religious assistants who dedicate their lives at the side of AIDS victims and take care of their families. He spoke of the precious services given by thousands of Catholic health institutions that in Africa help all those stricken by AIDS, malaria or tuberculosis. "My appeals have not been in vain," he added. "I note with satisfaction that numerous countries and institutions support and coordinate their efforts — concrete campaigns of prevention and care to sick persons."

Prayer of Pope [St.] John Paul II to Mary

16. With AIDS patients

> O Mary, Immaculate Virgin, turn your maternal gaze especially on those who, in Africa, are in extreme need because they are stricken with AIDS or other mortal disease.
>
> Look upon the mothers who weep for their children; see the grandparents deprived of sufficient resources to support their grandchildren who become orphans.
>
> Hold all of them in your maternal heart, Queen of Africa and of the whole world. Virgin most holy, pray for us.

[For the World Day of Prayer for the Sick, 11 February 2005]

APPENDICES

The Struggle for the Gospel of Life

As long as God allows me to live, I will reject any behavior that leads to AIDS; but, as long as God gives me the strength, I will care for AIDS patients with the love He has shown to me.

Man is foolish, illogical, egocentric; that is not important, love him anyway!

If you do good, you will be accused of egoistic intentions; that is not important. Do it well!

If you achieve your objectives, you will find false friends and true enemies; that is not important. Achieve them!

The good you do will be forgotten tomorrow; that is not important. Do it well!

Honesty and holiness make you vulnerable; that is not important. Be loyal and honest!

What you have taken years to build up can be torn down in an instant; that is not important. Build it anyway!

If you help people, they will be angry with you; that is not important. Help them!

Give to the world the best of yourself and it will mistreat you; that is not important. Give the best of yourself!

These words of Mother Teresa, pronounced in 1990, direct all our actions in our SELF organization. If it is useful to promote national campaigns of prevention, nothing can replace close contact to bring complete and precise information on the reality of HIV but also to testify to escorting sick persons and show the face and the concrete reality of this pandemic.

Throughout the diverse and numerous interventions in parishes, Christian communities who receive us and the schools of religious instruction, we propose a teaching in the awakening of compassion, of love, of the meaning of life, of sharing to the young audience that we meet. Our message is still the Gospel of Life to change our outlook and open our hearts so as to receive the message of life, love, mercy, and compassion that we can prove to our neighbor in need. May we able to say, like St. Peter of Alcantara who responded to a lord who was complaining that everything was going badly: "Make a good heart for yourself; this will be one part of the world that will go well."

Bibliography of French works omitted.

Fr. Thomas McGlynn, OP

Printed in Great Britain
by Amazon